What people are saying about *Raw and Radiant*

"Gorgeous recipes that taste as delicious as they will make you feel. You don't have to be a raw foodist or vegan to appreciate these simple, gratifying meals."

—**Michelle Branch,**
Singer, songwriter

"Summer is a raw food goddess and her recipes are out of this world! She has been my go-to-girl for amazing raw recipes and inspiration for several years now. Summer has truly mastered the raw lifestyle and makes eating live, vibrant food fun and delicious!"

—**Whitney Tingle,**
Cofounder of Sakara Life

"I feel so fortunate to have the pleasure of knowing and working with Summer Sanders. She is a unique talent that truly inspires. Her passion behind health and living foods is genuine—her vibrancy transpires into the food that she makes, as well as the people she is around. Both she and her book are gorgeous! Get the book to get the vibe! You will love it."

—**Meredith Baird,**
Author of *Coconut Kitchen* and founder of Nucifera

RAW AND RADIANT

130 QUICK RECIPES AND HOLISTIC TIPS FOR A HEALTHY LIFE

SUMMER SANDERS

Skyhorse Publishing

Photographs on pages 11, 23, 207, 226, 232, 235, 243, 244, and 250 by Lauren J. Schumacher
Photographs on pages 161 and 230 by Summer Sanders
Photograph on page 240 by Jane Ferrel
All other photographs by Alexa Gray
Food Styling + Creative Direction: Summer Sanders

Skyhorse Publishing books may be purchased in bulk at special discounts for sales promotion, corporate gifts, fund-raising, or educational purposes. Special editions can also be created to specifications. For details, contact the Special Sales Department, Skyhorse Publishing, 307 West 36th Street, 11th Floor, New York, NY 10018 or info@skyhorsepublishing.com.

Skyhorse® and Skyhorse Publishing® are registered trademarks of Skyhorse Publishing, Inc.®, a Delaware corporation.

Visit our website at www.skyhorsepublishing.com.

10 9 8 7 6 5 4 3 2

Library of Congress Cataloging-in-Publication Data

Names: Sanders, Summer (Nutritionist), author.
Title: Raw and radiant : 130 quick recipes and holistic tips for a glowing
   life / Summer Sanders.
Description: New York, NY : Skyhorse Publishing, [2018] | Includes
   bibliographical references and index.
Identifiers: LCCN 2017039123| ISBN 9781510724747 (hardcover : alk. paper) |
   ISBN 9781510724754 (ebook)
Subjects: LCSH: Raw food diet. | Raw food diet--Recipes. | Raw foods. |
   Self-care, Health.
Classification: LCC RM237.5 .S27 2018 | DDC 641.3/02--dc23 LC record available at https://lccn.loc.
gov/2017039123

Cover design by Jane Sheppard
Cover photograph by Alexa Gray

Print ISBN: 978-1-5107-2474-7
Ebook ISBN: 978-1-5107-2475-4

Printed in China

My son Henry, may you always know where your true home is.
To my husband Mike, thank you for loving every meal I make.
Mom and Tim, thank you for teaching me the beauty and power of plants, healthy foods,
and heart connection. Wherever I am, I know I'm okay. Thank you for this.

CONTENTS

INTRODUCTION

MY STORY

I've had a love for holistic health, plant-based eating, and fitness for as long as I can remember. It has long been a passion that has become my purpose. I was born in the Ozarks of Missouri, on a self-sustainable 10-acre farm; my father is an organic farmer and my mother is a Waldorf educator as well as a total health nut. They raised me to be aware of the food I eat, where it comes from, and most importantly, how to heal myself and my family with it. Growing up with wheatgrass-shooting, carrot juice-drinking, big salad-consuming parents set a foundation that I am eternally grateful for. **No matter where I've been or how far down the rabbit hole I went, I knew where home-base was in my body and in my heart.** I knew what healthy felt like and I knew how to get back there. Growing up with these amazing people has been a major influence on where I am today and what I feel passionate about sharing.

Like many, I strayed from the path I was shown growing up. After leaving my little sleepy town of Sedona, I lived in Los Angeles and San Francisco. I worked in the music and beauty industries, which both can be very high-stress with late night parties, very hectic coffee-powered days, and not much time for one's self. I was sick often, tired, extremely drained, overweight, and felt no willpower or drive within myself. Caught in cycles of toxic relationships and not seeing my true essence, I got very depressed. A deeper place within me knew there was another way to make it in the world, another way to live, but I felt so helpless and bogged down by the weight of worldly expectations. I attribute my reawakening to a book called *The Presence Process*, which found its way to me in early 2009. This book was what I needed to give me a little bit of a shake and a major wakeup call.

The summer of 2010 was a very transformational time for me. A lot had happened in my life in a very short time—I got married, my husband left for an eleven-month deployment to the Middle East, I quit drinking, I began reading books that supported a positive way of living, I started a consistent meditation practice, I began to listen to my body again, I began practicing yoga, and I also went 100 percent raw. For the first time in a long time, I felt a deep sense of purpose and gratitude. I also felt like I needed to share some of the things that woke me up out of my sleep—thus, *Raw and Radiant* was born.

All that pain, passion, and experience led me to open Local Juicery in 2014. Local Juicery is an organic, plant-based kitchen and pressed juicery located in Sedona, Arizona.

We opened a second location in early 2017. Local has furthered my education and respect of whole, plant-based raw foods and given me an incredible platform to share my love of great food, cleansing, and juice.

I'm so happy to be able to share my recipes and health tips with you! Let's dive in.

How This Book Can Help You

Adopting an abundance of raw, plant-based food into your diet is such an amazing way to support your body, mind, and spirit. This book will help you learn the foundations of live food prep, the value of gentle cleansing, how to eat with the seasons, what foods to eat in moderation, workouts that help you lose fat and gain energy, beauty foods that will boost your glow from the inside out, and supportive tips for a radiant life. *Raw and Radiant* is not just a recipe book, it's a great resource for making lasting changes that will truly support your whole self. I see it as a comprehensive holistic health guide that will help you live healthy, wake up energized, and really get that glow.

Raw and Radiant has five parts, starting with **The Basics**. Here I will cover the basics of raw food cuisine, why I love plant-based eating, what you need for preparation, supplements, and my ultimate grocery list. Part two is where the fun really begins, **The Recipes,** where I'll share my favorite breakfasts, nut milks, smoothies, soups and salad, dressings and sauces, main dishes, sweet treats, and juices! You'll be amazed with how quickly you can make these scrumptious raw food recipes and with how easy it is to add them to your diet. You'll be set with a raw recipe for every occasion—berry cheesecake for a birthday, pizza for the kids, juices for cleansing, smoothies for on-the-go, I got you covered. Part three is all about **Cleansing**. Perfect for getting your body cleaned out and ready for real food, or just for a gentle maintenance cleanse. This detox section covers common questions and concerns about cleansing as well as recipes and a daily plan. The last section of the book is what I call the keys to a **Holistic Lifestyle**—fitness, beauty, nurturing passions, rituals, entertaining in the raw, and helpful mantras to keep you centered, glowing, and healthy. Lastly, you'll find the **Appendices,** which include plenty of helpful info on soaking and sprouting, making flour, and additional reading and resources. These resources will help you be successful on your raw food journey and give you tools that will make recipes in the book and others easy, nutritious, and delicious!

PART I.
BASICS

THE RADIANTLY RAW LIFE

MY FOOD PHILOSOPHY

Each of us must make our own choices regarding our health, diet, and lifestyle. We are unique and lovely creatures with many complexities that must be considered. What to eat can get incredibly confusing, especially these days. There are so many diets and so many advocates for them: Paleo, raw, vegan, pescatarian, ketogenic, bulletproof, 80/10/10, and so on. This is a big reason I rely on intuitive eating, simply listening to the body's needs and following my intuition when it comes to food and simple health. I personally don't identify with any particular diet; I'm an equal opportunist and enjoy food so much! I always have a pastry when at Tartine in San Francisco, I love the experience of fine foods, I love good traditional pizza, and I don't have any unhealthy restrictions. I don't eat extravagantly every day, because it's just not what my body craves anymore. Indulging every now and then is a part of my life, but what I have found works best for me is to relax into the simplicity of the food that the earth provides—unprocessed, organic, raw food. I eat this way most of the time and I feel amazing, and maintain a healthy body and a positive mind.

I believe food should be fun and it should make you feel alive; it shouldn't be something that is scary, intimidating, or overthought about. Keeping it simple keeps it elegant.

BENEFITS OF A RAW, PLANT-BASED DIET

A diet rich in raw foods is a way of eating that respects your body, respects the earth, and respects other living beings. Eating limited meat and dairy also happens to be incredibly beneficial to your health and longevity. A raw focused, plant-based diet is filled with nutritionally dense foods that are easily assimilated into the body and used for its optimal functions. Raw food is technically not heated over 118 degrees (some raw food enthusiasts only heat their food to 105 degrees)—this preserves important enzymes and nutrients that are often lost when the same foods are cooked. By eating foods in their raw form, you are feeding your body vibrant, alive foods that will nurture and energize your whole being. Cooked foods can be void of many enzymes and nutrients and our bodies have to work harder to digest them. We do have some enzymes in our body that help break down food, but in today's world of fast-paced jobs, polluted air, and dirty water, many of these natural enzymes the body should be producing are not functioning at their optimum levels or are no longer produced when needed. Enjoying a lifestyle that includes an abundance of raw plant-based foods can help your body absorb the nutrients from the food, repair itself, glow from head to toe, and ultimately heal much faster.

WHY RAW FOOD?

Raw food changed my life, my body, and my self-concept. I know many people who share the same experience, who in some way were awakened by this way of eating and have made plant-based foods a staple for themselves and their families. Eating a wholesome diet with emphasis on raw foods has been known to cure irreversible diseases, help people lose and actually keep off weight, as well as support emotional awareness in mind, body, and soul. I lost twenty pounds when I started including more raw foods in my diet. My mind cleared up, I was able to focus and actually get things done. My follow-through, commitment, and excitement for living skyrocketed. I had an amazingly positive experience from simply changing the way I fed my body. My clients have had very similar experiences by doing raw cleanses, detoxing, and adding more plant foods into their diets. I have so much love for the simplicity of raw food and all that can be learned and gained from it.

I know quite a few people who adapted to a raw food diet due to extreme health issues like cancer and heart disease. Kris Carr, author of *Crazy Sexy Diet* was diagnosed with a rare incurable cancer at the age of thirty-one. She has successfully kept her cancer "sleeping" naturally with no medical intervention for the past thirteen years. She did this with a combination of raw organic foods, green smoothies, spiritual practice, and positive lifestyle changes. She is the poster child for raw food and it's healing powers.

Ageless Beauty and Longevity

Many people are intrigued by eating raw because it's known to provide clear skin, bright eyes, weight loss, and high energy. Eating foods in their raw form can absolutely help you get that dewy glow and a nice trim body, but I think you'll find as you go deeper that the benefits go far beyond the exterior. There is nothing more beautiful than a person who truly knows themselves and is willing to

"The whole process of digestion is related to our appearance. The manifestation of our genetic and spiritual blueprint is a result of whatever we eat, assimilate, and eliminate."

—David Wolfe,
Author of *Eating for Beauty*

go to the not-so-pretty places within. Cleansing your body can bring you to a place of self-acceptance and real beauty. When you cleanse your body, you can't help but begin to cleanse the mind.

Longevity is another common reason I hear why people decided to add more raw foods to their diet. Mimi Kirk, a long time raw foodie and author of *Live Raw,* is a stunning blond with vibrant eyes and healthy skin—you would never guess she's in her seventies.

She looks like a radiant woman, who maybe is in her fifties. She's a great example of aging gracefully on a raw food diet with none of the debilitating diseases or symptoms common in seventy-year-olds these days. We want to live and we want to live long, healthy, vibrant lives. Plant-based eating is a great way to make this happen.

When I'm eating a diet rich in raw foods, I am awake, vibrant, energized, excited, and I'm in love with life. I feel incredibly motivated, activated, and connected. I love how my body responds to eating raw, fresh, organic foods. I lose my winter layer of fat around my thighs and midsection, my eyes are bright, and my skin is flawless. These are many of the reasons that I lean heavily on raw food. I don't eat raw 100 percent of the time, I'm not dogmatic in my approach, but no other way of eating has ever felt as natural and good to me as a vibrant raw diet. Raw foods play a huge part in my life and my family. My little boy is a fan of spinach, chard, and spirulina at the tender age of three! I know this is because he sees his mom and dad eating real food. Nothing means more to me than to pass this on to our next generation.

By adding more radiant and raw roods to your diet, you will have fewer cravings, your body will be alkalized, you'll be well-hydrated, you'll digest your food easier, your body will assimilate the nutrients in your foods better, your hormones will balance out, you'll be energized, your immune response will be stronger, you'll lose weight, and you'll look and feel younger. I always tell my clients that are skeptical of eating a predominately raw diet to give it one month and if they don't feel a significant change in their body and mood, then I will not charge them for my services. I've yet to not get paid. The great thing about raw food is that you don't have to eat a 100 percent raw diet to get the benefits. By adding at least one raw meal a day to your diet you will be well on your way to feeling some of these great benefits that a diet rich in plant-food provides.

Healthy Food, Busy Life

I've created recipes that will help you get a radiant glow and will still support a busy and flourishing life. Many people feel intimidated by raw foods and lifestyle changes because of the time commitment. I'm a mama to the busiest boy in the world, I run two cold-pressed juice bars, write for my websites and businesses while managing multiple social media accounts; my time is precious. This book is for people like me, who want to thrive without spending every waking moment in the kitchen and at the gym. The majority of the recipes in this book only require you to have a high-powered blender and a small food processor. The recipes are designed for people on the move, who want to fuel their bodies with the best food possible. I've also added in some extremely easy meal ideas that don't require any electronic tools at all, just a cutting board and a good chef's knife. My hope is to make raw food accessible to everyone, everywhere, all the time.

Reclaiming Your Intuition

I wrote this book for everyone, not just hardcore raw foodies. My hope is that someday everyone will have the knowledge to be able to benefit from the healing powers of a plant-based diet. I neither expect nor necessarily suggest that you eat 100 percent raw. I am a big advocate for intuitive eating. By tuning into our bodies and building a relationship with them, we can begin to understand what they need. Our bodies are miraculously designed and have the capabilities to communicate their needs to us. In order for our bodies to communicate properly, they must be as clean as possible, otherwise you might interpret the body's message as "I need sugar" or "I need cheese" when really the body is just asking healthy fats or a deep green juice. Confusing at first, but after a while you'll be speaking your body's language flawlessly.

Below, I have listed some foods and substances that I feel are important to take a close look at in order to reset your body to a super clean and intelligent state. By adding (and taking away) some of these, you will begin to transform your relationship and understanding of your body. This will help you know which foods are best for you and how you should eat for your unique system. I also have included a five-day juice and smoothie detox in this book (page 226) to help you gently cleanse your body. This cleanse, along with considering some of these adjustments, will help you reset and support you to start eating intuitively.

My Principles of Health: What To Kick and What to Keep

Everything in moderation—I don't like to feel restricted. I've found that if you tell yourself "no," you can't have something, then it's likely that is all you will be able to think of. I support enjoying life fully and sometimes this means you eat the piece of cake with buttercream icing. I know my body can handle a treat like that every so often because most of the time I stay within close range to these pillars of health below. Start slowly, remove one at a time.

Alcohol

Studies have shown that long-term alcohol consumption leads to fat gain, stresses critical internal organs, and keeps us from optimum health. I don't think we need studies to tip us off to the not-so-glamorous side of cocktails. Drinking creates ashy skin, bloodshot eyes, dehydration, and regretful mornings. If you want to have a drink, a glass of organic, or even better, biodynamic wine is a great way to kick back and relax. Organic red wine does have some health benefits, but many take it beyond the glass. I understand it's hard with holidays, birthdays, and social events. What I suggest is to consider not making every occasion about drinking. There are plenty of other ways to enjoy life, such as family time, outdoor sports, fitness classes, dance classes, cooking together, games, photography, and educational workshops, etc. It has become wildly acceptable to go out and drink three times a week, for some even more. Take a break, try a month with no booze, and see how you feel. Watch your motivation soar and your body come alive again.

Sugar

Most of us now know processed sugar is bad for our bodies and can be detrimental to health and wellness. We have plenty of alternatives such as unprocessed Stevia, xylitol, dates, or raw honey. Sugar is addictive and so it's often really hard for people to kick the habit.

Do not ever, under any circumstances, use artificial sweeteners, it's like health suicide. Many of the artificial sweeteners like aspartame contain phenylalanine; phenylalanine turns into diketopiperazine, a known carcinogen. When processed by our bodies these chemicals turn into formaldehyde. Clearly, you don't want that in your body. As natural health expert Dr. Mercola states: Ultimately, aspartame will be fully absorbed into your body. Ten percent of what is absorbed is the breakdown product methanol (wood alcohol). The EPA defines safe consumption of this toxin as 7.8 milligrams a day, which is the amount found in about half a can of diet soda.

These artificial sweeteners are cancer causing* and degrade long-term health. It's hard to cut out sugar for many of us because we've become dependent on it. It feeds the yeast in our body and the moment we quit, the detox symptoms can be overwhelming. Push through and lean on natural sugars while you are cleansing off of refined sugars. The benefits of going sugarless outweigh the shortly-lived high.

> "It's as addictive as nicotine or heroin—and as poisonous, responsible for modern plagues ranging from depression to coronary thrombosis.
> It's sugar."
>
> —William Duffy, author of *Sugar Blues*

Coffee

Coffee is a really hard one for people to give up, myself included. I still enjoy coffee once in a while, but only in moderation and only when it's organic. Coffee stresses the system, can drain the adrenals and give a deceptive feeling of energy that ultimately leads to a crash. It creates a dependency and causes headaches and irritability when trying to quit. I suggest lessening your intake and considering other sources of caffeine besides coffee. Some of my favorite alternatives are dandelion tea, yerba mate, and matcha. If you follow me on instagram (@summer.sanders) you'll see me posting my matcha lattes on the daily! Dandelion tea is a rich, full-bodied herbal tea that tastes very similar to coffee and can be made into fabulous lattes. It's also known to help with the withdrawal symptoms many experience when quitting coffee. Yerba mate has caffeine in it but is much mellower than coffee, it only contains 85 milligrams in eight fluid ounces, compared to the 200 in a cup of coffee. Yerba mate has been proven to be beneficial for your body and does not drain your adrenals. It gives you an even energy boost without the dreaded five o'clock crash, thanks to the theobromine, xanthines, and theophylline found in the leaves. Green tea or matcha also contains caffeine but it is very low, only 35 to 50 milligrams per eight fluid ounces. Green tea is known for its healing and age-defying properties, as well as having high amounts of antioxidants, fighting fatigue, helping with weight loss, and bad breath.

Coffee is very acidic and in my opinion, if you are working on healing from any form of cancer or even the common cold, you should stop drinking it immediately. Overly acidic bodies tend to take longer to heal. Replace with one of the substitutions above. Make sure to check out my blog www.strongandradiant.com for recipes that include these lovely options.

*[source] Bowen, J., Aspartame Toxicity and Methanol, Ethanol, Pectin, Methyl Alcohol, http://www.321recipes.com/aspartame.html

Overeating

Let's face it, we as a nation are addicted to food. Food has the power to heal, but it also can be detrimental when abused. People have a tendency to eat more than their body needs. This can be harmful to your inner organs and to your waist line. It's important to be mindful of your body when eating, especially when consuming heavy foods. Keep portions in check when it comes to foods such as sugar, dairy, flour, nuts, and seeds. These foods are harder on your digestive system and are best used in moderation. Nuts and seeds are a predominant part of raw food cuisine and consuming them is important, but just remember that they are a higher fat food and the body will take more time to break them down. Make sure to soak and sprout them when possible (see section on soaking and sprouting on page 245), as this will help diffuse the phytic acid and make them easier to digest. As with anything, use common sense and enjoy these heavier foods in a balanced way. Enjoy eating with your full body, not just your emotions and taste buds!

Supplements + Healthy Tips

These are the supplements that assisted me on my health journey and continue to be a part of my daily routine. I recommend them for all my clients and feel that they play an important part in overall health. I'm not a doctor, but in my experience these supplements are worthwhile and beneficial to everyone, raw foodie or not!

Enzymes

You hear the word enzymes tossed around a lot these days, especially when talking to raw foodies and vegan health nuts like me! Here are the enzyme basics so you can partake in the next conversation you overhear at your favorite juice bar.

Enzymes are one of the most important components in our bodies. Enzymes are what allow us to digest and break down our foods. Enzymes are involved in almost every chemical action in our bodies. We were all born with the ability to produce enzymes; we began our lives with a stockpile! However, the Standard American Diet (often referred to as SAD) has used up many of our enzyme stores without replacing them. When we eat foods that are heated over 118 degrees, our bodies are forced to make enzymes instead of using the ones that naturally occur in uncooked foods and, unfortunately, most peoples' bodies and diets are devoid of the minerals needed in order to produce these enzymes. Dr. Edward Howell states in his book *Enzyme Nutrition,* "Length of life is universally proportional to the rate of exhaustion of the enzyme potential of an organism. Increased use of food enzymes promotes a decreased rate of exhaustion of the enzyme potential of an organ. Increased use of food enzymes promotes a decreased rate of exhaustion of the enzyme potential." When the food we eat demands and drains the enzyme reserves, the body is unable to produce enough enzymes to repair damage or break down food. This is often why people supplement their diet with store-bought enzymes such as bromelain.

Enzymes and Cooked Food

If you are eating a primarily plant-based diet with emphasis on raw foods, chances are you're getting a multitude of live enzymes. When foods are cooked, the naturally occurring enzymes are killed off. The longer the food is cooked, the more enzymes die. Some foods can actually benefit from being lightly steamed, but for the most part if you are eating cooked foods, I strongly suggest supplementing with digestive enzymes to support nutrient absorption and proper digestion. I always have enzymes available. When you first start adding more raw foods to your diet, you might find that you are bloated and have a hard time digesting your food. This will pass—in the meantime, use your digestive enzymes to aid your body in the process. Follow the directions on the brand that you choose.

Probiotics

Essentially, a probiotic is a bacterial culture that is taken to support run-down intestinal populaces. They are good bacteria that our bodies need to keep the intestines healthy and our immune function up. Like enzymes, we're born with probiotics in our body (they live in the small and large intestines), but many of the foods, medicines, antibiotics, chemicals, and even the air we breathe kill these friendly bacteria and leave us ill-equipped to fight off common colds and sickness. In my opinion and experience, good health begins in your gut and I choose to supplement with a probiotic in pill and food form. You can find probiotics at your supermarket in pill form, or in a liquid form. It is also possible to get probiotics from foods such as fermented coconut water, fermented veggies, and yogurt.

Colon Therapy

Colon therapy sounds like something you would want to run away from, I get it! It's not the most appealing thought, but this form of cleansing can have amazing health benefits that far outweigh the general discomfort we have with discussing our bowels. In my experience and observations as a health coach, a healthy colon very often equals a healthy person.

"The colon is a very changeable and susceptible part of the body. An injury, surgery, or other stress such as emotional upset or negative thinking can alter the flora."

—Robert O. Young, PhD, DSc, author of *Sick and Tired?*

There are colon therapists that you can go to that will help guide you through the process or you can buy an enema bag and do the clean out yourself. Someone who is just starting a healthy eating lifestyle could really benefit from weekly self-given enemas (see page 223), but if you have been on a healthy kick for a while, you might consider seeing a professional. Enemas can only do so much, but colonics can really get further into the colon and remove waste that could be undermining your health.

Vitamin B12

Many vegans, vegetarians, and raw foodist do not get enough Vitamin B12 in their daily diet. The lack of this vitamin can cause energy loss and fatigue. Vitamin B12 is typically found in meat and can also be taken in pill or shot form. If you decide to take a pill or shot, make sure to research the brand and ingredients.

The best source of natural vegan Vitamin B12 is wheatgrass and barley grasses. Wheatgrass contains every vitamin in the B-complex family. You can also get vitamin B12 from some Kombuchas and it's found sometimes in nutritional yeast. It's especially important to make sure you get a daily dose of Vitamin B12 when you are pregnant or nursing.

Lemon Water

This is so simple, yet very effective. It is one of the things that I do consistently, even when I am not following a perfect diet. It has many healing properties and nutritional benefits:

- Boosts your immune system
- Balances pH levels
- Aids in digestion
- Helps with problem skin
- Helps with adrenal fatigue
- Helps cleanse liver and kidneys
- Soothes acidic stomach

If you're traveling or not able to get to warm water, it's fine to use lukewarm room temperature water. It's also fine to use limes when lemons are not available.

SUPERFOODS

Another term you probably hear at the juice bar. Superfoods are plant foods that are incredibly high in nutrients. You can eat a very small amount of superfoods, and still get a whole lot of health benefits. They are loaded with antioxidants, minerals, protein, and more! Below I've listed some of my favorite superfoods and a little bit about the benefits of each. I use some of these wonder foods in my recipes, but you definitely don't need to stock up on all of these at once! Most natural food stores carry superfoods in bulk, but if your local health food store doesn't, check out sunfood.com

Maca Root is a root that originated in South America. It's well known for its hormone balancing properties as well as being a natural stimulant. It's great for libido and both male and female reproductive organs. This is one superfood that I suggest consuming cooked. Raw maca is very high in yeast and mold, and is hard for your body to digest. I suggest buying a roasted maca that is easier for the body to digest.

Lucuma is a native fruit of the Andes. It is known as a low calorie, low glycemic sweetener. It's also a wonderful source of fiber, vitamins, and minerals. Lucuma is high in beta-carotene, iron, and niacin.

Cacao has more antioxidants than any other known food. It is rich in minerals, incredibly high in vitamin C, and full of fiber. It also is a great natural source of serotonin and tryptophan.

Goji Berries, also known as the wolf-berry, have been used in Asian herbal medicine for years. The goji berry contains high-quality protein, healthy fats, and soluble fiber. It is packed with eighteen amino acids (including all eight essential amino acids). This little berry is high in vitamin A, loaded with trace minerals and vitamins including iron, phosphorus, zinc, riboflavin, vitamin E, and carotenoids. Goji is a powerful and delicious superfood that can easily be used everyday.

Spirulina is a type of blue-green algae that is rich in protein, vitamins, minerals, carotenoids, and antioxidants that help protect cells from damage. It is a great source of protein that is easily absorbed by the body.

Camu Camu is the name of a bush that grows in the rainforest of Peru. It bears a fruit called Camu Camu as well. The fruit is high in amino acids and higher in vitamin C than any other known fruit in the world. It is a mood lifter, hormone balancer, and an immune system booster.

Hemp Seeds are nature's perfect protein. Raw organic hemp seeds are a great source of nutrition and energy. They contain all the essential amino acids, making them a complete protein. They meet over a quarter of the RDA's daily fiber needs per spoonful. Raw hemp seeds are rich in minerals and full of vitamins.

Açaí has up to thirty times more anthocyanin than red wine and is very high in antioxidants. Acai helps promote general well-being, energy, stamina, and mental clarity. It is also great for lowering bad cholesterol.

Mesquite is a high protein traditional Native American superfood. Filled with calcium, magnesium, potassium, iron, and zinc, and rich in the amino acid lysine, mesquite adds a rich flavor to nut milks and smoothies.

Reishi is a medicinal mushroom, often used in powdered form. It offers inducible support to the brain and the immune system.

CBD oil is delivered from hemp and offers a calming and anti-inflammatory effect on the body. It is just now starting to get a lot of love in the natural healing community. I use 2rise Naturals and enjoy the calming and healing effects daily.

Pine Pollen is a natural source of testosterone that supports both male and female hormonal balance. It's high in B vitamins and also contains a host of minerals such as calcium, copper, manganese, magnesium, iron, and phosphorus.

Matcha is powdered green tea and is incredibly high in antioxidants, making it a superfood for anti-aging and fighting free radicals. It is a great way to start the morning with a little caffeine and no jitters.

THE DETOX EFFECTS

When you begin a raw food cleanse and start detoxing your diet, you will experience a lot of wonderful things, such as weight loss, a clear mind, and loads of natural energy. At the same time, something to be aware of is the emotional and physical detox that often takes place when you decide to clean up your lifestyle. Detoxing in essence is your body letting go of all the toxins, fats, chemicals, sugars, and emotional repression that have been building up for years. Not many consider cleansing a desirable state, but if you can find a way to "be with" what you're going through and stay

"If you don't think your anxiety, depression, sadness, and stress impact your physical health, think again. All of these emotions trigger chemical reactions in your body, which can lead to inflammation and a weakened immune system. Learn how to cope, sweet friend. There will always be dark days."

—Kris Carr,
author of *Crazy Sexy Diet*

present with your experience, the detoxing symptoms will eventually pass and you will be more likely to stick to your newfound healthy lifestyle. I also want to note that you may feel extremely happy and light—some of us tend to repress our happiness and good feelings because somewhere along the way we learned it wasn't okay to be joyful. When we start letting go of layers, it frees up this happiness to come out.

The point of cleansing is to renew yourself and to toss out the residues of unhealthy living, physically, emotionally, and mentally. Some may ask how emotions play a part in cleansing and diet—your emotions have much to do with how you eat, when you eat, and what you choose to eat. Many of us (especially women) tend to eat out of stress, sadness, loneliness, and boredom, and often feel guilt, shame, and fear around food. We eat unconsciously and feed ourselves for reasons other than true hunger. Eating disorders are very common these days, and have a lot to do with deeper emotional layers that coincide with diet and food. When you start to take a deeper look at the underlying emotions you carry around diet and food, you'll most likely uncover some very interesting and important information about yourself and your habits. There is a great book out on the mind-body health connection called *Mind over Medicine* by Doctor Lissa Rankin. In this book, Doctor Rankin gives scientific proof that you can heal yourself and change your life by changing your mind, and therefore your emotions. I recommend it to anyone wanting to learn more about mind-body connection and how to heal yourself naturally. Another great program for those who need support with food and emotions in Gabrielle Bernstein's *Finally Full*.

At times during your detox you might feel more sensitive than usual. Trust yourself, trust the process and the emotions, it is all happening for a reason. Stay with it; let yourself feel what may surface without judgment, the key is self-forgiveness. If you fall off the wagon for a moment and eat something that you've decided isn't included in your new lifestyle, let it go! It's all good, let it go and jump back on. It's only your mind that keeps you from success. Don't sweat the small stuff. Shaming yourself for eating something not included in your "diet" is not what we're after here, support yourself in being loving and making decisions based on that love is what it's all about. You might find that what you have spent time on in your life no longer seems very interesting or engaging. You begin seeing life from a different angle, and your thoughts become more keen and flexible.

When we care for ourselves and choose what is really right for our unique body, mind, and spirit, others who are close to us and used to our old way of living might become confused or uncomfortable. They may not understand why you don't want to party late, eat cheese plates, and blow through bottles of wine (that's a peek into my old lifestyle). When we make a change for the positive, it can feel to our friends like we are looking down on them if they don't do as we do. A true friend will love and support you through your changes. They will see the positives and even if they don't jump on board, they will cheer you on. You may lose a friend or two, but when one door closes another opens. Make room for the beauty that will surely enter into your life. Of course you can continue to care about others who are unsure about the changes they see in you. In my experience, the most meaningful way you can show your love for these people is by showing up for yourself and setting a positive and purposeful example. Don't forget the power of one!

Detox Symptoms

Below are some examples of physical detox symptoms you might experience (usually no longer than 3–4 days). Please do not let these deter you from cleansing; they are only possibilities and the degree to which you experience them is dependent on your past life style.

- Skin breakouts
- Bloating
- Stomach pains
- Headaches
- Intense food cravings
- Trouble sleeping, nightmares
- Diarrhea and constipation
- Fatigue, drowsiness, low energy levels
- Irritability
- Congestion or mucus that feels like a cold

STOCKING YOUR KITCHEN

In order to make the *Raw and Radiant* recipes, you will need some basic kitchen tools and appliances. Below are the tools that I suggest you have in order to easily make the recipes in my book. Most of these can be purchased online or at your local kitchenware store. Stores such as Williams Sonoma and Sur la Table will have most everything you need. A spiralizer is a unique tool that turns veggies into noodles, and is so much fun to experiment with! These can be bought on Amazon for a very reasonable price.

What You Need:
Chef knife
Glass containers or jars with lids for storing nuts, seeds, and powders
Glass containers with lids for storing prepared foods
Glass jars with lids for soaking
Box grater

High-powered food processor
Large cutting board
Mandoline for slicing veggies
Nut milk bag or cheese cloth
Paring knife
Spiralizer
High-speed blender such as a Vitamix
Dehydrator (most of the recipes in this book do not require one)

THE MARKET EXPERIENCE

I have provided a grocery list below that will be incredibly helpful in stocking your healthy pantry. Even if you are not making all the recipes, you will do yourself a huge favor by having these products and foods ready and available in your home. They are health food staples and will set you off in the right direction. Remember, what you have around is what you'll turn to, so make sure it's healthy, organic, and minimally processed.

My Ultimate Shopping List

FRUITS

Blueberries
Strawberries
Raspberries
Apples
Bananas
Kiwis
Lemons
Limes

Oranges
Mangos
Papayas
Grapes
Grapefruit
Dates
Figs

VEGETABLES

Kale
Butter lettuce
Spinach
Chard
Collard greens
Carrots
Dandelion greens
Beets

Red bell peppers
Sprouts
Broccoli
Cauliflower
Tomatoes
Sweet peas
Yellow squash
Oyster mushrooms

Zucchini
Avocado
Garlic
Onion

Sweet potato
Cabbage
Radish
Portobello mushrooms

OILS

Extra-virgin cold pressed coconut oil
Extra-virgin cold pressed olive oil
Avocado oil

Raw sesame oil
Cold pressed flax oil
Hemp seed oil

HERBS, SPICES & MORE

Sea salt
Ginger
Turmeric
Cumin
Garlic granules
Celery seed
Vanilla extract

Cinnamon
Sauerkraut
Greek olives
Maca root
Organic non-GMO chickpea miso
Maine Coast organic nori

NUTS & SEEDS

Raw organic almonds
Raw organic hazelnuts (filberts)
Raw organic cashews
Raw organic pecans
Raw organic walnuts
Raw organic macadamia nuts
Raw organic hemp seed

Raw organic chia seeds
Raw organic sunflower seeds
Raw organic pumpkin seeds
Raw organic sesame seeds
Raw organic almond butter
Raw organic coconut butter
Young coconuts

SWEETENERS

Stevia (I love Omica Organics)
Organic raw coconut palm sugar
Pure maple syrup

Raw local honey
Coconut nectar

MISCELLANEOUS

Organic buckwheat groats
Organic oat groats
Cacao nibs
Cacao powder
100% organic cranberry juice

Nutritional yeast
Lecithin (sunflower)
Psyllium husk
Organic flax seeds

EATING WITH THE SEASONS

The ingredients you use to make your food will influence the flavor and outcome of the recipes. When available, try your best to only use organic, local, and sustainable foods. I like to eat with the seasons; this way the majority of the food I'm eating was grown near me. I feel that nature knows best; eating watermelon in the middle of winter just doesn't feel right. Here is a simple guide to eating with the seasons. Farmers' Markets and small local grocery stores often only have seasonal ingredients available.

Spring
Artichokes, arugula, watercress, asparagus, mustard greens, dandelion greens, baby spinach, parsley, baby carrots, baby chard, fennel, nettles, peas, radishes, ramps, morels, beets, navel oranges, cherries, strawberries.

Summer
Avocados, basil, beans, beets, blackberries, blueberries, boysenberries, cantaloupe, chilies, cilantro, corn, cucumber, eggplant, grapes, nectarines, okra, peaches, peppers, plums, raspberries, watermelon, zucchini.

Fall
Apples, pears, Brussels sprouts, winter squash, pumpkin, persimmons, garlic, carrots, kale, chard, broccoli, cauliflower.

Winter
Broccoli rabe, sweet potatoes, carrots, onions, garlic, kale, rutabaga, parsnips, turnips, sunchokes, beets.

"The food you eat can be either the safest and most powerful form of medicine, or the slowest form of poison."

—Ann Wigmore, holistic health practitioner and raw food advocate

PART II. RECIPES

Here is the fun part! The food. . . . One of my main goals when writing **Raw and Radiant** was to provide you with accessible and practical ways of preparing raw, plant-based cuisine. The recipes and techniques I've included will help you incorporate more plant-based raw food into your kitchen, while providing inspiration for your own creations. These recipes are merely guides. Ultimately, you should use your personal preferences to make the recipes work best for you. I encourage you to learn the basics, then have fun and play with this wonderful way of eating.

The recipes were designed for busy people with busy lives. I've kept the majority of the recipes to a twenty-minute prep time or less. The ingredients required for the recipes are readily available at your local natural food store and won't break your bank account. I've also made sure that most of the recipes don't require a dehydrator. This can make raw food so much easier. All you really need is a high-speed blender and a food processor. I know that when I'm busy running around the last thing I want to do is have to plan and think about a meal two days ahead of time. This is great for special occasions, but for everyday life, it's just not realistic. I hope you enjoy these simple, yet delicious recipes that I've developed for you. Have fun and enjoy!

BREAKFAST

What you put into your body first thing in the morning has the power to set the tone for your whole day. In our fast-paced culture, many people turn to sugary cereals, processed carbohydrates, overly acidic coffee drinks, and hard-to-digest animal proteins that just so happen to be quick and convenient. Breakfast should leave you feeling energized, healthy, and ready to face the day. When you start your day with fresh, plant-based, easy-to-digest foods, you will begin the day in a light and energized way. You'll feel activated and ready to go! The recipes in the breakfast section are great for everyone—for the athlete, the mom on the go, the busy dad, the children, and the whole family. Enjoy these delicious and vibrant plant-based raw breakfasts.

MY MORNING TONIC

sex drive, energy, antioxidants

This is my go-to breakfast—I make a version of this every day. Sometimes it's warm and based in tea or organic coffee. I add lots of different superfoods and herbs based on what I'm feeling my body needs. This blend is amazing for the brain, the female sex organs, and anti-aging. Ashwagandha is one of the incredible energy-giving ingredients, great for balancing adrenals while also giving you horsepower! Enjoy this energetic blend.

Serves 2–3

What You'll Need
2 cups Almond Milk (page 58)
2 heaping tablespoons almond butter
1 tablespoon coconut butter
1 tablespoon raw organic goji berries
2 tablespoon raw cacao powder
½ teaspoon ashwagandha
½ teaspoon reishi
1 tablespoon favorite vegan protein powder
¼ teaspoon sea salt

Method
Combine almond milk, butters, goji, cacao, ashwagandha, reishi, protein, and salt in your blender. Blend until frothy and delicious. Pour and enjoy!

Coconut Cream Coffee

energy, focus, metabolism boost

I love to enjoy this recipe when I'm on a coffee week (I tend to cycle on and off). Find what works for you with coffee and give this a try for a decadent and motivating morning drink. I use a French press, which preserves the amazing oils that are in coffee. Skip the frappe, guys—this is where it's really at. Nutritious without the high sugar. I love Omica Organics, my favorite Stevia of all time.

Serves 1–2

What You'll Need
12 oz organic single-origin brewed hot coffee
1 tablespoon coconut butter
1 teaspoon coconut oil
1 tablespoon maple syrup or raw honey
5-8 drops of vanilla Stevia
1 pinch cinnamon

Method
Blend the coffee, coconut butter, oil, maple syrup, sweetener, and cinnamon on high in your high speed blender. Serve with a dash of cinnamon on top. For an even more indulgent morning, add a tablespoon of raw cacao!

BALANCED GRANOLA

sex drive, fiber, antioxidants

This is a fabulous recipe for balancing hormones and energizing the body. The superfood Maca is an adaptogen that helps the body find its balance and stabilize its hormone production. I always suggest this recipe to clients who are just getting off of synthetic birth control pills, or for men who are feeling that their testosterone levels aren't where they should be. This cereal can be stored in the freezer and keeps for at least a month. It's great served with almond milk and berries. I also love taking it on the road with me when I'm traveling.

Serves 4

What You'll Need
1 banana
2 cups raw almonds
1 cup raw pecans
⅔ cup shredded raw organic coconut
⅓ cup raw organic goji berries
3 tablespoons raw organic hemp seeds
½ tablespoon maca powder
½ teaspoon vanilla extract
1 tablespoon cinnamon
¼ cup coconut oil, not melted
½ teaspoon sea salt
½ cup maple syrup or raw honey

Method
In a large bowl, combine the banana, almonds, pecans, coconut, goji berries, hemp seeds, maca, vanilla, cinnamon, coconut oil, salt, and sweetener, and mix everything up really well. You may want to glove up and use your hands to really get the consistency good.

Set your dehydrator to 118 degrees and let it heat up. If you don't have a dehydrator, you can still make this recipe, just set your oven at the lowest temperature and preheat.

Spread mix onto Teflex sheets or, if you're using the oven, a cookie sheet.

If dehydrating, it will take 12–15 hours until it's crunchy and ready to go. If baking it will be 30–45 minutes.

Coconut Cream Parfait

probiotics, fiber, antioxidants

This recipe takes a bit of time to prepare because of the coconut yogurt fermentation, but it's well worth it. The yogurt is full of probiotics; this is an ideal recipe for those who are transitioning to raw. It goes nicely with the Balanced Granola (page 37), but is wonderful with berries and bananas as well.

Serves 4

What You'll Need

Yogurt

3½ cups young coconut meat

1 cup soaked cashews

½ cup coconut water

1 teaspoon powdered vegan probiotic

1 tablespoon lemon juice

1 teaspoon vanilla extract

2 tablespoons raw honey

¼ teaspoon sea salt

Toppings

1 cup Balanced Granola (page 37), optional

½ cup fresh strawberries, raspberries, or blueberries

Method for Yogurt

Blend the coconut meat, cashews, and coconut water in a high-speed blender until very creamy. Add the vegan probiotic and blend until combined. Some coconut meat is very moist, while other coconuts have drier meat and will need liquid added. Transfer the coconut mixture with a plastic or wooden spoon into a glass bowl and cover with a clean cloth. Set the bowl in a dehydrator at 105 degrees overnight. If you don't have a dehydrator, you can leave the yogurt out in a warm part of your house, but be aware that it may need a little more time than the dehydrated version. Check it for a slight sour smell; this is how you know it's ready.

If you don't have access to coconut meat, you can use all soaked cashews instead, following the same process and measurements.

After the yogurt is dehydrated, add the lemon juice, vanilla, honey, and sea salt. Whisk or blend until well incorporated.

Assembly

Place the yogurt into the bottom of a glass jar, tumbler, or bowl. Layer with granola and your choice of superfoods, fruit, or nuts.

THE BEST AÇAÍ BOWL EVER

antioxidants, omegas, immunity

Açaí bowls are a fabulous breakfast, lunch, or dinner. At my home, we eat them at all times of the day. They are filling, energizing, and actually very low in sugar. This recipe features banana and avocado, but if you are looking for a lower glycemic version, you can simply omit the banana and add a bit of Stevia to taste. You can typically find raw frozen Açaí in the frozen section at your local natural food store.

Serves 1–2

What You'll Need

¾ (3.5-ounce) packets frozen Açaí
1 medium frozen banana
¼ medium ripe Hass avocado, pitted and peeled
1 cup Almond Milk (page 58)
1 tablespoon vanilla Sun Warrior Protein Powder or favorite raw protein powder (optional)
2 tablespoons almond butter
¼ teaspoon sea salt
½ cup organic shredded coconut
⅓ cup goji berries
½ cup fresh berries of choice
1 teaspoon bee pollen
drizzle of raw honey

Method

In a high-speed blender combine the Açaí, frozen banana, avocado, almond milk, protein, almond butter, and salt. Blend until the mixture is a smooth, pudding-like consistency. If the mixture is too thick to blend easily, add a little more almond milk. Once the mixture is blended, transfer to a bowl and top with shredded coconut, goji berries, fresh berries, bee pollen, and drizzle with honey.

Sexy Superfood Cereal

fiber, antioxidants, natural energizers

A couple of years ago we visited some friends in Nantucket who were raw foodists. I was at the beginning of my 100 percent raw journey and still learning a lot. Our host made a breakfast that was similar to this one, and at the time it blew my mind! I had been eating very simply and this was a true food experience for me. To this day I continue to make it and every time I do, I'm never let down.

This is a great breakfast for kids too! You can make it omitting the maca for children. Maca can affect hormones, and for children it is not needed or suggested. You could replace it with mesquite or lucuma.

Serves 2

What You'll Need
½ cup raw organic Brazil nuts
½ cup raw organic unsalted pistachios, shelled
¼ cup raw organic hemp seeds
5 dates, pitted and chopped
3 tablespoons goji berries
1 teaspoon ground cinnamon
1 teaspoon maca powder
¼ teaspoon sea salt
Fresh fruit of choice
Nut milk of choice

Method
In a food processor, blend the Brazil nuts, pistachios, hemp seeds, dates, goji berries, cinnamon, maca powder, and salt, leaving it a bit chunky. Serve over fruit with your favorite nut milk. This cereal will keep in the freezer for three months. Store in glass container with a tight-fitting lid.

BLUEBERRY OVERNIGHT OATS

protein, fiber, healthy fats

Overnight oats are a busy mom's best friend. They are amazing because you literally just put everything in a jar at night, set it in the refrigerator and by morning you have the perfect breakfast for you and your family. This version includes chia, which is one of my personal favorite superfoods for energy and a sustained fullness.

Serves 2

What You'll Need

1 32-ounce mason jar
24-oz Almond Milk (page 58)
1 banana
2 tablespoons raw honey or maple syrup (sometimes I use 7 drops of Stevia for a
　　low glycemic option)
¼ teaspoon salt
cinnamon to taste
2 tablespoons almond butter
¼ cup chia seed
1 cup of gluten-free rolled oats
¼ cup blueberries
½ cup raspberries
½ cup hemp seeds

Method

Blend almond milk, banana, sweetener, salt, cinnamon, and almond butter together in your high-speed blender. Pour chia into the bottom of a mason jar. Pour ⅓ of the almond milk mixture over the chia, stir and then layer with oats. Pour another ⅓ cup liquid, then layer with fruit and hemp seeds, pour more liquid, and continue layering until finished. Let set overnight or for at least 1 hour.

Decadent Pecan Pancakes

antioxidant, omegas, fiber rich

This is a bit of a longer recipe, simply because it does have to be dehydrated, but I couldn't leave it out. It's an amazing play on raw foods and so, so, so enjoyable. I love it layered with fruit and coconut butter whipped with honey or simply on their own. My son Henry loves these so much. I make a huge batch and keep them in the refrigerator for snacking—they taste like banana bread!

Serves 2

What You'll Need
2 medium ripe bananas
½ cup Almond Flour (page 247)
½ cup pecans, soaked
¼ cup cashews, soaked
I tablespoon vanilla
2 tablespoons chia seeds
¼ teaspoon salt
½ cup water

Method
In your high-speed blender or food processor (for a more rustic texture as pictured), combine bananas, flour, pecans, cashews, vanilla, chia, salt, and water. Use a spatula to scrape all of the mixture from the container and put into a medium mixing bowl.

Set dehydrator for 118 degrees and portion out your pancakes using a ⅓ cup for each onto Teflex sheets. Smooth out the pancakes into round 4x4-inch circles using a small spatula or the back of a spoon. Dip the spoon or spatula in water if you find it getting sticky.

Dehydrate for at least 6 hours, then flip off of Teflex sheet and let the other side dehydrate for another 4.5–6 hours (less if in dry climate). When done they should not be gooey, but firm and a little flexible.

POWER CHIA PORRIDGE

fiber, vitamin C, energizers

This is an amazing energizer. My husband is an athlete and a former Naval Special Warfare Officer. When he was on deployments in the Middle East, chia was one of the staple foods that I would send him. It keeps you hydrated, full, and energized, and doesn't require much to prepare. This recipe is the ultimate power breakfast or pre/post gym meal. It's guaranteed to fill you up and keep you moving.

Serves 2

What You'll Need
2 cups Almond Milk (page 58)
½ medium banana
1 teaspoon vanilla extract
2 dates, pitted and chopped
¼ teaspoon sea salt
¼ cup raw organic chia seeds
½ cup goji berries
¼ cup raw organic hazelnuts
1 teaspoon maca powder
1 teaspoon lucuma powder
½ teaspoon camu camu powder
1 cup fresh fruit of choice

Method
In a high-speed blender, combine the almond milk, banana, vanilla, dates, and sea salt. Blend until smooth. Pour the mixture into a bowl and add chia seeds. Whisk and then let sit for at least 20 minutes, remembering to stir periodically.

In a food processor, combine the goji berries, hazelnuts, maca, lucuma, and camu camu. Pulse to mix. Be careful not to overwork the mixture, pulsing until well incorporated but still crumbly.

Pour the chia mixture into a bowl and top with dry mix and fresh fruit.

BERRY CHIA CREAM BREAKFAST PUDDING

So obviously I like chia—I just love how easy it is and how many options there are! This is an amazing breakfast or even a dessert. By blending the chia you create a creamy pudding that is really delicious and great for little ones. I love this recipe with the Balanced Granola (page 36) on top, as pictured.

Serves 4

What You'll Need
½ cup chia seeds
3 cups Almond Milk (page 58)
1 large banana, peeled
2 heaping tablespoons raw honey
4 tablespoons cashew butter
1 ½ cups raspberries, fresh or frozen
1 teaspoon vanilla extract
¼ teaspoon sea salt
¼ cup coconut flakes
favorite berries for topping

Method
Mix chia and almond milk in a bowl and let sit for 30–45 minutes for maximum deliciousness. Stir the mixture every 10 minutes or so, so that it doesn't clump.

In a high-speed blender combine banana, raw honey, cashew butter, raspberries, vanilla and sea salt. Blend on high until smooth and creamy. Once you have the right consistency, transfer to a bowl and stir in chia mixture. Top with favorite berries and coconut flakes.

To make this recipe creamy as pictured, just blend the chia mixture in with all the other ingredients.

MATCHA CHIA PUDDING

protein packed, antioxidants, fiber

This is by far my favorite chia pudding that I've ever tasted. The maple syrup makes it so delicious—you have to taste it to see what I mean. You can always opt for a lower sugar version by using Stevia instead. I use Omica Organics Vanilla, or Butterscotch flavor and it works well in this recipe. I like it sweet so I use ½ dropper. This recipe is really lovely when layered with your favorite superfoods or nuts in a glass jar or cup. It keeps really well too. Matcha is my absolute favorite superfood and energizer. Great for anti-aging, energy, and overall a good mood food.

Serves 4

What you'll need
2 cups creamy Cashew Milk (page 69)
⅓ cup maple syrup
¼ cup almond butter
4 tablespoons matcha powder
1 teaspoon vanilla extract
¼–½ teaspoon sea salt
½ cup chia seeds
1 cup sprouted and dehydrated almonds for layering
1 medium banana

Method
In a high-powered blender, combine the cashew milk, maple syrup, almond butter, matcha powder, vanilla, and salt. Pour into a bowl after it has blended and add all of the chia. Whisk and let set for at least 20 minutes.

To assemble, layer with almonds and sliced banana.

TURMERIC VANILLA COCONUT PUDDING

healthy fats, anti-inflammation, hormone balancing

Turmeric is my favorite superfood—I love the flavor, I love the color, I love the benefits. The black pepper in this recipe is to support the bioavailability (how much of the nutrients your body can actually absorb and use) of the turmeric. You can, of course, play with this recipe and add berries or other fun flavors in place of the turmeric if you want to change it up. I love using persimmon when the season is right!

Serves 2

What You'll Need
2½ cups young coconut flesh
¼ cup soaked cashews
½ teaspoon turmeric powder or 1 small thumb fresh turmeric
½ cup Almond Milk (page 58)
½ ripe Hass avocado
5 dates, pitted
1 teaspoon cinnamon
1 teaspoon maca powder
¼ teaspoon pine pollen
1 teaspoon vanilla extract
¼ teaspoon black pepper
½ teaspoon sea salt

Toppings
½ banana, sliced
1 tablespoon coconut shreds
1 teaspoon bee pollen (optional)

Method
In a high-speed blender, combine the coconut flesh, cashews, turmeric, almond milk, avocado, dates, cinnamon, maca, pine pollen, vanilla, black pepper, and salt. Blend until very creamy, adding more almond milk if needed.

Once it is incredibly well blended, top with bananas, coconut shreds, and bee pollen.

CRUNCHY CLASSIC GRANOLA

antioxidants, fiber, brain support

This is a really tasty, high-protein cereal. Buckwheat is a wonderful gluten-free grain alternative. Its robust flavor blends well with the banana and cinnamon, making it a delightful way to start the morning. This simple, sophisticated cereal is very easy to make and has only a few ingredients. I enjoy this cereal most with my Pecan Milk (page 61). It's great for adults, wonderful for children, and sure to impress even your most picky friends and family. If you don't have a dehydrator, you can make this recipe in the oven on the lowest setting; it won't be technically raw, but it will still be a wonderfully healthy breakfast option.

Serves 4

What You'll Need
1 large banana
½ teaspoon sea salt
1½ teaspoon ground cinnamon
1½ cup gluten free rolled oats
1 cup hemp seeds
¼ cup dried blueberries, or dried berry of choice
1 cup chopped pecans

Method
Combine the banana, salt, and cinnamon in a high-speed blender and blend until smooth. Transfer the banana mixture to a bowl, and add the rolled oats, seeds, and dried berries of choice. Stir until well-combined, then spread the mixture on a Teflex sheet and dehydrate overnight at 115 degrees (bake on low for 45 minutes if you don't have a dehydrator). It might come out a bit clumped, so go ahead and break it into bite-sized pieces. This cereal keeps really well in the freezer or in a sealed jar.

NUT MILKS

If you are trying to cut dairy out, you bought the right book—I have a slight obsession with nut and seed milks, and they are so tasty and nutritious. My milk recipes are perfect for children's cereals, coffee, tea, and smoothies. My husband drinks the Almond Milk by the gallon, literally! The basic process of making the milks is all the same. Put the ingredients in a blender, blend on high for two minutes, strain with a nut milk bag, and serve. I store mine in big mason jars or old glass milk bottles. The milk keeps for three to four days. Always label them with the date you made them. One key thing to remember is if you are soaking your nuts and seeds for longer than 8 hours, transfer them to the refrigerator. This will keep your nut milks fresher for longer.

ALMOND MILK

alkalizing, protein packed, mineral rich

Almond milk is very alkalizing for the body. It's wonderful on its own or as a base for smoothies, puddings, and desserts. This recipe calls for lecithin, which is a stabilizer that helps keep the milk from separating. If you don't have lecithin, it's fine; the recipe will still turn out wonderfully.

NOTE: A nut milk bag or fine strainer is needed for straining.

Serves 6

What You'll Need
1½ cups soaked organic raw almonds
4 cups filtered water
1 tablespoon vanilla extract
3 tablespoons coconut nectar
¼ teaspoon sea salt

Method
Blend the almonds with the water in high-speed blender for two minutes, then strain. Pour the strained milk back into the blender with the vanilla, coconut nectar, and salt. Blend until well mixed, then pour into a glass container. Refrigerate for 10–15 minutes to cool, then serve.

Store in a glass jar with a tight-fitting lid. This milk will keep in the refrigerator for four days.

Sesame Seed Milk

bioavailable calcium

Sesame seeds are full of calcium, magnesium, zinc, fiber, phosphorus, and iron. They are so tasty and nutritionally dense. Studies have shown that sesame seeds can lower blood pressure and help protect the liver. They are also known to help with headaches, PMS, and menopause.

Did you know that sesame seeds actually have more calcium then milk? If this is hard for you to believe, then I think those "'Got Milk?" ads might have gotten to you. Sesame seeds have 1404mg of calcium per cup. Milk, on the other hand, only has 276mg of calcium per cup. Clearly, we've been a bit misinformed. Sesame is the way to go for strong, healthy bones.

Serves 6

What You'll Need
1½ cup raw sesame seeds
4 cups filtered water
1 teaspoon vanilla extract
10 dates, pitted
½ teaspoon sea salt
1½ teaspoons cinnamon

Method
Blend the sesame seeds with the water in a high-speed blender for two minutes, then strain. Pour the milk back into the blender with the vanilla, dates, and salt, and cinnamon. Blend until smooth. Pour the milk into a glass container and refrigerate until cold. Serve chilled.

Store in a glass jar with a tight-fitting lid. This milk will keep in the refrigerator for four days.

MATCHA MILK

anti aging, plant protein, energizing

Matcha is one of my favorite flavors. Whenever I'm off coffee, I typically rely on matcha for a nice solid energy. Matcha is a great source of antioxidants and really supports the body in repairing its cells. I personally love the flavor and use it in many of my recipes.

Serves 6

What You'll Need

4 cups unsweetened Cashew Milk (page 69)

4 cups unsweetened Coconut Milk (page 64)

½ teaspoon vanilla extract

¼ cup plus 1 tablespoon matcha powder

½ cup maple syrup

½ teaspoons sea salt

Method

Blend together the unsweetened mylks, vanilla, matcha powder, maple syrup, and sea salt. Get it nice and frothy! If you would like to enjoy this recipe warm, just warm on your stove top!

PECAN MILK

zinc, heart healthy, vitamin E

When I came up with this recipe and drank it for the first time, I remember thinking that nobody has lived until they've tried Pecan Milk. It's heavenly! You're in for a treat.

Serves 6

What You'll Need

1 cup soaked raw organic pecans

4 cups filtered water

½ teaspoon vanilla extract

1½ tablespoons organic maple syrup

¼ teaspoon sea salt

Method

Blend the pecans with the water in a high-speed blender for two minutes, then strain. Pour the strained milk back into the blender with the vanilla, maple syrup, and salt. Blend to combine, then pour into a glass container and refrigerate to cool before serving. Store in a glass jar with a tight-fitting lid. This milk will keep in the refrigerator for four days.

HOLY HAZEL

| alkalizing, protein packed, healthy fats |

Hazelnut milk is great for people who are busy because you don't have to soak raw organic hazelnuts. Their skin doesn't have the enzyme inhibitors that most nuts carry. Just throw them in, and blend.

Serves 6

What You'll Need

1 ½ cups raw organic hazelnuts

4 cups filtered water

½ teaspoon vanilla extract

2 tablespoons coconut nectar

¼ teaspoons sea salt

Method

Blend the hazelnuts with the filtered water in a high-speed blender for two minutes, then strain. Pour the strained milk back into the blender with the vanilla, coconut nectar, and salt, then blend again. Pour the milk into a glass container and refrigerate to cool before serving. Store in a glass jar with a tight-fitting lid. This milk will keep in the refrigerator for four days.

QUICK HEMP MILK

| omegas, complete protein, healthy fats |

This is a great on-the-go milk! It takes less than two minutes to make and you're on your way. A great one for children and for athletes, loaded with healthy bioavailable protein. I lived on this when I was pregnant.

Serves 6

What You'll Need

4 cups filtered water

1 cup hemp seeds

3 tablespoons raw organic almond butter

3 tablespoons raw honey

½ teaspoon sea salt

Method

In a high-speed blender, combine the water, hemp seeds, almond butter, honey, and salt and blend on high until smooth. Store in a glass jar with a tight-fitting lid. This milk will keep in the refrigerator for four days.

Raw Creamer

alkalizing, protein packed, fiber-rich

This is an amazing thick milk that can be used for coffee, tea, or the base of homemade ice cream. By using less water and adding macadamia nuts to the mix it creates the perfect creamy milk.

Serves 4

What You'll Need
1 cup soaked raw organic almonds
¾ cup soaked raw organic macadamia nuts
6 dates, pitted
4 cups filtered water
½ teaspoon vanilla extract
½ teaspoon sea salt

Method
Blend the almonds, macadamia nuts, and dates with the water in a high-speed blender for two minutes, then strain. Pour the strained milk back into the blender with the vanilla, and salt. Blend until well combined, then pour into a glass container. Refrigerate to cool before serving. Store in a glass jar with a tight-fitting lid. This milk will keep in the refrigerator for four days.

Coconut Milk

fat burner, energy, protein

Coconut milk is an amazing base for soups, smoothies, and really good for just drinking on its own! Coconut has many healing powers, but one of the coolest things about coconuts is that it's a medium chain fatty acid; less medium chain triglycerides (fatty acids) are converted to fat than longer fatty acids. These MCTs enter your blood stream quickly and are taken directly to the liver, where they are used as an immediate source of fuel for the body instead of being stored as fat—one of the many reasons to enjoy coconuts guiltlessly.

Serves 6

What You'll Need
1 ½ cups coconut flakes
4 cups filtered water
1 teaspoon vanilla extract
1 tablespoon coconut oil
4 tablespoons coconut nectar
¼ teaspoon sea salt

Method
Blend the coconut with the water in a high-speed blender for two minutes, then strain. Pour the coconut milk back into the blender. Add the vanilla, coconut oil, coconut nectar, and salt, and blend until smooth. Pour the milk into a glass container and refrigerate to cool. Serve chilled. Store in a glass jar with a tight-fitting lid. This milk will keep in the refrigerator for four days.

Goji Milk

This is a really fun milk that I loaded with antioxidants. I love using this as a smoothie base or just drinking it on its own. The color is so beautiful.

Serves 6

What You'll Need
4 cups of your favorite nut milk (my favorite is almond)
¼ cup raw organic goji berries, soaked
3 tablespoons raw honey
1 tablespoon cinnamon
1 tablespoon vanilla
½ teaspoon sea salt

Method
In a high-speed blender, combine the nut milk, goji berries, honey, cinnamon, vanilla, and salt. Blend until smooth and well combined. Strain the mixture, then transfer to a glass container and refrigerate to chill before serving. Serve cold. Store in a glass jar with a tight-fitting lid. This milk will keep in the refrigerator for five days.

Chocolate Milk

You can make this chocolate milk with any milk. I prefer making it with a creamier nut milk for taste and consistency. For a wonderful vegan hot chocolate, heat it slowly on the stove while stirring frequently. I like adding some immune boosting superfoods like reishi mushroom powder from SunPotion.

Serves 6

What You'll Need
4 cups Almond Milk (page 58) or Walnut Milk (page 69)
½ cups raw organic cacao powder
¼ cup organic maple syrup
1 tablespoon vanilla extract
½ teaspoon sea salt

Method
Blend the almond milk, cacao powder, maple syrup, vanilla extract, and salt in a high-speed blender for two minutes, then strain into a glass container and refrigerate for 15 minutes to cool. Serve chilled. Store in a glass jar with a tight-fitting lid. This milk will keep in the refrigerator for four days.

SUNFLOWER HEMPSEED MILK

omegas, protein packed, calcium

This milk is so creamy and full of flavor. It's my favorite milk to use in smoothies and in desserts. It's very much like rich, full-fat cow's milk. Raw organic sunflower seeds are very high in vitamin E, a fat-soluble antioxidant that has anti-inflammatory properties, as well as helping to prevent cardiovascular disease. Raw organic sunflower seeds have also been known to lower bad cholesterol, calm nerves, and improve detoxification. Hemp is a complete protein, high in magnesium, zinc, and healthy omegas. Hemp has all the essential amino acids and is made up of 65 percent globulin edistin. Globulin edistin is a protein that is only found in raw organic hemp seeds. It helps with digestion, immunity, and stress.

Serves 6

What You'll Need
1 cup raw organic sunflower seeds
¾ cup hemp hearts
6 cups water
1 teaspoon vanilla extract
10 dates, pitted
½ teaspoon salt

Method
Blend the sunflower seeds and hemp with six cups of water in a high-speed blender for two minutes, then strain. Pour the strained milk back into the blender. Add the vanilla, dates, and salt and blend until smooth. Pour into a glass container and refrigerate to cool. Serve chilled. Store in a glass jar with a tight-fitting lid. This milk will keep in the refrigerator for four days.

WALNUT MILK

brain power, heart health, cancer fighter

I find it fascinating that walnuts are so good for our brains and also happen to look like a brain. I love this milk for its earthy flavors and full-bodied creamy texture. Wonderful for kiddos, too!

Serves 6

What You'll Need
1 cup raw organic walnuts

4 cups filtered water

1 teaspoon vanilla extract

¼ cup organic maple syrup or raw honey

½ teaspoon sea salt

Method
Blend the walnuts with the water in a high-speed blender for two minutes, then strain. Pour the strained milk back into the blender. Add remaining ingredients, and blend until smooth. Store in a glass jar with a tight-fitting lid. This milk will keep in the refrigerator for four days.

CREAMY CASHEW MILK

magnesium rich, copper, cancer fighter

This is one of my favorite indulgent milks; it's great for smoothie bases and for anything chocolate-based. On top of being super creamy and delicious, it also has some great health advantages. Cashews contain proanthocyanidins, a form of flavanols that starve tumors and stop cancer cells from multiplying. That's right, drink up!

Serves 6

What You'll Need
1 cup raw organic cashews

4 cups filtered water

1 teaspoon vanilla extract

3 heaping tablespoons raw honey

½ teaspoon sea salt

Method
Blend the cashews with the water in a high-speed blender for two minutes, then strain. Pour the strained milk back into the blender. Add the vanilla, raw honey, and salt. Blend well, then pour into a glass container with a tight-fitting lid. This milk will keep in the refrigerator for four days.

Spirulina Milk

Almond milk is one of my favorite things. Spirulina is one of the healthiest things. It made sense to put them together. At first, I wasn't sure if this combination would work out. Spirulina can have a strong flavor. I played with the recipe and found what I think is the perfect ratio. Spirulina is a great source of bioavailable protein, iron, and vitamin E. I love this mixture and even put it in my coffee or matcha.

Serves 4

What You'll Need
1 cup raw organic almonds
4 cups filtered water
5 tablespoons raw honey
1 tablespoon spirulina
Pinch of sea salt

Method
Blend the almonds with the water in a high-speed blender for two minutes, then strain. Pour the strained milk back into the blender. Add the raw honey, spirulina, and salt. Blend until smooth, then pour the milk into a glass container and refrigerate until cold. Serve chilled. Store in a glass jar with a tight-fitting lid. This milk will keep in the refrigerator for four days.

SMOOTHIES

Smoothies are an easy and delicious way to get vital nutrients, especially for those of us on the go! When I'm working long hours and traveling, I rely on these organic blended fruits, veggies, and superfoods to make sure I get what my body needs to sustain me. I even travel with a small blender—it might seem obsessive to some, but I know what my body needs to stay healthy and to stay true to my lifestyle.

The basic smoothie contains a base, a core, and enhancers. A base typically will determine the texture of your smoothie; you can use nut milk, juice, coconut water, or even just water. The core will determine the flavor, such as strawberries, mango, or bananas. Some of my favorite enhancers are spinach, spices, or superfoods. Green smoothies have become super popular as of late and for good reason—they are a wonderful way to get all your nutrients in one cup.

Have fun, create, and be healthy.

SMOOTHIE BUILDING

Base
This is the base of your smoothie: Great liquids for raw vegan smoothies are coconut water, coconut milk, fresh pressed fruit juice, fresh pressed veggie juice, nut milks, and even water.

Core
This will decide the overall taste of your smoothie. It's nice to have a fruit that is a little heavier. Some of my favorites are bananas, mango, papaya, berries, persimmons, pears, and citrus.

Enhancers
This is where you can add in some great nutrients without overpowering the taste. Smoothies are a clever way to give children great nutrition.

Kale, spinach, chard, and lettuce are some great greens for smoothies.

Other favorites include cacao powder, raw organic almond butter, spirulina, maca, coconut manna, and all other superfoods to make your smoothies unique and flavorful!

Hippie Hemp Smoothie

protein, amino acids, manganese

This smoothie is based on hemp milk. Hemp seeds are incredibly nutritious, offering complete protein and omegas 3-6-9. During my pregnancy, my main source of protein was hemp. It's a tasty and powerful little seed. I love to include it in almost all of my meals and smoothies.

Serves 1

What You'll Need
2 cups Quick Hemp Milk (page 62)
1 large frozen banana
1 medium date, pitted
1 cup tightly packed fresh spinach
¼ cup organic hemp seeds
2 tablespoons cacao powder
¼ teaspoon sea salt
1 teaspoon cacao nibs, for topping

Method
In a high-speed blender, combine the hemp milk, banana, date, spinach, hemp seeds, cacao, and salt. Blend on high until smooth and creamy. Add a few ice cubes if it doesn't taste cold enough for you. To serve, pour into glasses and top with cacao nibs.

RADIANT SKIN SMOOTHIE

illuminating, hydrating, enzyme rich

Radiant, glowing, lustrous skin. This super smoothie contains some of the best ingredients for your skin to thrive. Hydrating coconut water, antioxidant-rich blueberries, enzyme-rich pineapple, and papaya and avocado that provide healthy fats. This smoothie also has tocotrienols, which is vitamin E. Vitamin E is an essential nutrient for the body and helps with anti-aging. You can buy tocotrienols at your local health food store or vitamin supplier. All these superfoods work together to get you the glow!

Serves 1

What You'll Need
2½ cups fresh young coconut water
¼ cup fresh or frozen papaya
¼ cup pineapple chunks
¼ cup blueberries
¼ ripe Hass avocado, pitted and peeled
2 teaspoons tocotrienols (see headnote)
¼ teaspoon sea salt

Method
In a high-speed blender, combine the coconut water, papaya, pineapple, blueberries, avocado, tocotrienols, and salt. Blend on high until smooth. Pour into glass to serve.

Summer's Morning Blend

free radical fighter, immune booster, natural energizer

This is a great morning smoothie, full of plant-based protein, antioxidants, healthy fats, and loads of bioavailable vitamins. This is what I call a whole food smoothie; it's much like a meal and actually can be used in place of one. It keeps you satiated, fueled, and ready for your day.

Serves 1

What You'll Need

2 cups young coconut water
½ large frozen banana
¼ cup fresh or frozen raspberries
¼ cup fresh or frozen strawberries
1 cup fresh spinach, packed tightly
1 tablespoon vanilla Sunwarrior protein powder,
    or your favorite raw vegan protein powder
1 teaspoon maca powder
1 tablespoon raw organic almond butter
¼ teaspoon sea salt

Method

In a high-speed blender, combine coconut water, banana, raspberries, strawberries, spinach, protein powder, maca powder, almond butter, and salt. Blend on high until smooth. Add a few ice cubes if desired to make it colder and thicker.

Strawberry Bliss Cooler

vitamin C, immune booster, iodine

Perfect for a hot day, picnic, or midsummer dinner party, this smoothie is a great alternative to a margarita or other alcoholic beverage and can also lend itself to being an adult beverage if you choose! Great for a pool party.

Serves 1

What You'll Need
2 cups coconut water
1 ½ cups fresh or frozen strawberries
3 tablespoons fresh mint, minced, or ½ dropper of mint oil
2 tablespoons lime juice
2 tablespoons raw honey, or 5 drops of Stevia
½ cup ice
½ teaspoon sea salt

Method
Combine coconut water, strawberries, mint, lime juice, sweetener, ice, and salt in a blender. Blend well and serve cold.

SNICKERDOODLE MILKSHAKE

levels blood sugar, medium chain fatty acids, brain food

I made this smoothie recipe up when I was training for my first marathon. I was running so much every day and needed something to fuel me and replace the nutrients that I was sweating out. This was the perfect blend! Incredibly tasty and loaded with dense nutrition that the body needs when training hard. The pine pollen is an optional ingredient; I use it to help keep my hormones naturally balanced and find it really helps my stamina when I'm working out a lot. I use Sun Potion brand.

Serves 1

What You'll Need

2 cups young coconut water

1 cup young coconut meat, packed tightly

1 tablespoon maple syrup

2 heaping tablespoon raw organic almond butter

½ teaspoon lucuma powder

¼ teaspoon pine pollen

½ teaspoon cinnamon

½ teaspoon mesquite powder

1 teaspoon vanilla extract

¼ teaspoon sea salt

Method

Blend coconut water, coconut meat, maple syrup, almond butter, lucuma, pine pollen, cinnamon, mesquite, vanilla, and salt in the high-speed blender and serve.

Coco Leche

This is one of my favorite smoothies! It's like ice cream. Young coconut meat and water are a superfood in their own right. You can spot the young coconuts by their white husk and pointed top. They can easily be purchased at Whole Foods or most Asian markets; you can also buy frozen coconut meat, which is suitable as well. The coconuts are fairly easy to open once you get the hang of it. I like to start by shaving off the husk around the top and then using a meat cleaver to pry open the little cap. YouTube has some great instructional videos if you get lost.

Serves 1

What You'll Need

2 cups young coconut water
1 cup young coconut meat, packed tightly
1 tablespoon raw honey
1 teaspoon maca powder
½ teaspoon vanilla extract
½ teaspoon salt

Method

Add coconut water, coconut meat, honey, maca, vanilla, and salt to high-speed blender. Blend on high. Serve and enjoy!

LEAN MEAN GREEN MACHINE

pure energy, heavy metal detoxifier, immune boost

Pure green energy! This is a great smoothie for any time of day. I personally prefer to drink it in the morning. It's very alkalizing for your system. Start the day off right by loading up on your greens. This smoothie is also great if you're feeling under the weather. It's easy to drink and will help your body's immune system recoup.

Serves 1

What You'll Need
2½ cups young coconut water
½ cups shredded Curly or Dino kale, stalks removed
1 cup fresh spinach, tightly packed
¼ cup cilantro
¼ cup cucumber, peeled and coarsely diced
½ frozen banana
¼ cup frozen blueberries
¼ teaspoon salt

Method
Add coconut water, kale, spinach, cilantro, cucumber, bananas, blueberries, and sea salt to your high-speed blender. Blend on high until smooth.

STOMACH SOOTHER

alkalizing, enzyme rich, potassium

This is a great smoothie for pregnant mamas who have issues with morning sickness—the ginger, papaya, and lemon all work in sync to help fight the nausea. It's also good for after a night of a few too many drinks!

Serves 1

What You'll Need

2 cups coconut water

1 tablespoon ginger, peeled and chopped

1/4 cup lemon juice

2 cups Hawaiian papaya, peeled, seeds removed, and coarsely chopped

2 vegan probiotic capsules

5 drops Omica vanilla Stevia

1 cup ice (optional)

Method

Add coconut water, chopped ginger, lemon juice, papaya, probiotic, Stevia, and ice to your high-speed blender. Blend until smooth. If you would like a less fibrous texture, strain with nut milk bag and serve.

POST WORKOUT FUEL

protein, fiber, healthy fats

This is a great post-workout smoothie. It's full of healthy fats and protein that will keep you full and your energy levels high. My husband is a huge fan of this shake.

Serves 1

What You'll Need

2 cups Almond Milk (page 58)

1 medium frozen banana

1/4 cup frozen pineapple chunks

2 tablespoons coconut butter

1 tablespoon vanilla Sunwarrior protein powder

1 teaspoon of Maca

1/4 teaspoon sea salt

Method

Add almond milk, bananas, pineapple, coconut butter, protein powder, maca, and salt to your high-speed blender. Blend on high and serve.

CHOCO-MACA-GOJI SHAKE

magnesium, minerals, protein

This smoothie is such a treat! I drink it for dessert but feel no guilt. Everything in it is so incredibly healthy. This is a great special treat for children, although I would suggest taking out the maca and replacing it with lucuma.

When I worked at Sedona Raw Café in high school, we made a shake that was similar to this one. It was one of the recipes that got me really excited about raw food! I was so excited that I could drink something that tasted this amazing, and it was good for me. It really changed my world. I'm forever grateful!

Serves 1

What You'll Need
2 cups Pecan Milk (page 61)
1 medium frozen banana
3 tablespoons raw organic cacao powder
2 tablespoons raw organic almond butter
½ teaspoon maca powder
1 tablespoon raw organic goji berries, plus 1 tablespoon for topping
1 tablespoon raw cacao nibs, plus 1 tablespoon for topping
½ teaspoon vanilla extract
¼ teaspoon sea salt

Method
Blend pecan milk, banana, cacao powder, almond butter, maca, goji berries, cacao nibs, vanilla, and salt in your high speed blender, until smooth. Top with cacao nibs and goji berries.

BEAUTY BOOSTER

vitamin A, vitamin E, vitamin C

This beauty shake is full of vitamins and omegas, amino acids, minerals, bioavailable proteins, and cytokinins (plant-based hormones that regulate growth and have anti-cancer, anti-aging, and anti-thrombolytic benefits in humans). It's guaranteed to keep you full, energized, and pretty from the inside out! This is one of my favorite morning elixirs. The beauty booster smoothie also has MSM in it, which is a powerful beautifying supplement that contains sulphur, often dubbed the beauty mineral. You can find MSM powder at your local health food store. If you can't find it locally, it's available online.

Serves 1

What You'll Need
1 cup young coconut water
1 cup carrot juice
1 cup young coconut meat, tightly packed
½ teaspoon ground cinnamon
½ cup frozen mango
1 tablespoon cold pressed flax oil
½ teaspoon MSM powder
3 tablespoons tocotrienols
¼ teaspoon sea salt

Method
Add coconut water, carrot juice, coconut meat, cinnamon, mango, flax seed oil, MSM, tocos, and salt to your high-speed blender. Blend on high until smooth. Add ¼ cup ice if you prefer a colder beverage. Serve and enjoy!

CITRUS FLAX CLEANSER

enzymes, probiotics, omegas 3-6-9

This drink is a no-joke cleanser. If you're struggling with constipation or not having enough bowel movements (a healthy amount is three per day), I suggest drinking this daily until you are regular and then using it to maintain as needed. Good health starts in the gut, and so does disease. If you can keep your intestines healthy, you will reap the rewards. I use psyllium husk in this blend. You can find it at your local health food store in the supplements department or online. It's a wonderful natural fiber that helps move things along in a gentle way.

Serves 1

What You'll Need
2 cups grapefruit or orange juice
3 tablespoons lemon juice
1 tablespoon coconut oil
1 tablespoon flax oil
2 tablespoons psyllium husk
2 probiotic capsules
5 drops Stevia

Method
Blend grapefruit juice, lemon juice, coconut oil, flax oil, psyllium husk, probiotic, and sweetener in your high-speed blender until smooth. If it's too thick for your taste, add ½ cup of water. Drink quickly! The psyllium will thicken if you wait too long! Drink up. Follow with a cup of fresh water to help move through the body.

THAT MINT CHIP LOVE

boost libido, kick-starts metabolism, magnesium rich

This is a great smoothie for people who are trying to get healthy, but don't want to give up the flavor! It's light, full of healthy superfoods, and sustains the body for hours! I love it. It reminds me of mint chip ice cream. You can order E3Live online or pick it up at your local natural food store. From www.e3live.com: "E3Live is a is an organic blue-green algae wild-harvested from Klamath Lake in Oregon, USA. It's a nutrient-dense superfood containing over 65 vitamins, minerals, amino acids, and essential fatty acids. This plant-based superfood is non-GMO, vegan, and a rich source of chlorophyll."

Serves 1

What You'll Need
2 cups young coconut water or Almond Milk (page 58)
½ tablespoon E3Live or spirulina
2 tablespoons raw cacao powder
I cup fresh spinach, packed tightly
I medium frozen banana
2 tablespoons raw almond butter
I ½ droppers mint (or peppermint) extract or oil
¼ teaspoon sea salt
I tablespoon cacao nibs for topping

Method
Add coconut water, E3Live or spirulina, cacao powder, spinach, banana, almond butter, mint extract, and salt a high-speed blender. Blend mixture on high until smooth. Add ¼ cup of ice if you prefer a colder beverage. Top with cacao nibs.

SOUPS & SALADS

Soups and salads make up 80 percent of my diet. They are quick to make, loaded with nutrients, and super tasty! I treat my soups like I treat my smoothies; I load them up with power foods that keep me full and get me through my day. Salads are a great way to get fiber, healthy fats, vitamins, and important nutrients. They don't have to be boring! Spice them up with your favorite herbs, veggies, fruits, and dressings.

CREAMY COCONUT CARROT SOUP

fiber, vitamin A, liver cleanser

This soup is based on one of the first raw recipes I came up with. I've tweaked it a bit since the beginning, but it remains a staple in my diet. It's filling and extremely flavorful. I prefer it served chilled.

Serves 4

What You'll Need

4 cups fresh carrot juice

2 cups fresh young coconut meat

2 dates, pitted

2 tablespoons coconut oil

1 teaspoon ground cinnamon, plus more for garnish

¼ teaspoon cardamom

1 small thumb fresh ginger

1 teaspoon salt

1 tablespoon lemon juice

Shredded carrot, for garnish

Method

In a blender, combine the carrot juice, coconut meat, dates, coconut oil, cinnamon, cardamom, ginger, salt, and lemon juice. Blend on high for 2 minutes or until creamy. Transfer to bowls, and top with the shredded carrot and a sprinkle of cinnamon.

CREAM OF CUCUMBER

hydrating, alkalizing, detoxifying

Savory, yet refreshing. This is a perfect cold soup for the summertime. I love the blend of creamy cashew milk and cucumbers. I used to love cream based soups; this one really reminds me of some of my old favorites.

Serves 4

What You'll Need
2 medium cucumbers, peeled and coarsely chopped
2 tablespoons lemon juice, divided
Pinch of sea salt
1 large ripe Hass avocado, pitted and chopped
3 cups unsweetened Cashew Milk (page 69)
3 tablespoons cold pressed organic olive oil
¼ small shallot, finely diced
3 dates, pitted
Truffle oil for topping (optional)

Method
In a bowl, combine one of the chopped cucumbers with half of the lemon juice and a pinch of sea salt. Toss to combine and set aside.

In your high-speed blender combine the remaining cucumber with the avocado, cashew milk, olive oil, shallot, remaining 1 tablespoon lemon juice, dates, and sea salt. Pour into a bowl; add the reserved cucumber mixture on top in a thick line. I like to add a little truffle oil to this recipe to make the flavor interesting. It goes really nicely with the cashew milk and shallot.

SWEET PEA SPRING SOUP

fiber filled, healthy fats, hydrating

My husband and I had dinner at the home of our good friends, Max and Clare. Clare had made an amazing summer sweet pea vegan soup. I was inspired by her to create a raw version. After a little experimenting, I came up with this recipe.

Serves 4

What You'll Need

4 cups shelled sweet peas or frozen peas
¼ medium shallot, minced
I small garlic clove, minced
I large ripe Hass avocado, pitted and coarsely chopped
I medium cucumber, peeled and diced
4 tablespoons cold pressed olive oil
I tablespoon raw honey
4½ cups unsweetened Almond Milk (page 58)
I teaspoon sea salt

Method

In a high-speed blender, blend all ingredients on medium, slowly moving up to full speed. If you want a very smooth soup, blend until desired smoothness is achieved. If you would like a more textured soup, blend for only fifteen seconds. Chill in refrigerator until ready to serve.

THE MOTHER SOUP

vitamins, mineral rich, protein filled

When I first went raw, this was one of my go-to meals. I was eighteen and worked at a little raw food cafe in Sedona, Arizona. They served a green soup much like this one there, and I remember living on it during my first few months of raw food. I love it; it's a great, hearty, and nutrient-dense soup. I also eat this soup whenever I'm feeling under the weather, it's very alkalizing and healing. I use a little Nama Shoyu in the recipe, which is a raw fermented soy sauce. If you don't want to use this, coconut amino is a great option as well.

Serves 4

What You'll Need
2 large ripe Hass avocados
2 cups filtered water
2 large cucumbers, peeled and coarsely chopped
2 cups fresh spinach, packed tightly
1 medium red bell pepper, cored, seeded, and coarsely chopped
3 spring green onions, minced
1 garlic clove, minced
2 tablespoons lemon juice
3 tablespoon raw organic tahini
3 tablespoons Nama Shoyu
4 dates, pitted
Dash cayenne pepper

Method
In a high-speed blender, combine avocado, water, cucumber, spinach, bell pepper, green onions, garlic, lemon juice, tahini, Nama Shoyu, dates, and cayenne. Blend on high for 30 seconds or until creamy. Transfer to bowls. Serve with a heaping spoonful of raw hummus and raw crackers. I also love sprinkling kale chips on this soup.

Pineapple Gazpacho

fiber filled, enzyme rich, vitamin C

I made this for a dinner party that my friends John and Susanne hosted. They are not raw foodists but appreciate gourmet, farm-fresh foods. This refreshing soup was a total hit at the party. It is best served chilled.

Serves 4

What You'll Need

2 medium ripe pineapples, peeled and coarsely chopped
1 small jalapeño, diced
4 medium cucumbers, peeled and chopped
1 large ripe Hass avocado, pitted and chopped
1 cup minced green onion
2 tablespoons apple cider vinegar
2 tablespoons organic cold-pressed olive oil
½ teaspoon sea salt
4 cups water, more as needed

Method

Layer the ingredients in your high-speed blender starting with the pineapple and jalapeño (take the seeds out if you are sensitive to spice). Add cucumber, avocado, onion, and vinegar, olive oil, and salt. Pulse to blend. Add water slowly. Be careful not to overblend—this soup should be a bit chunky. Transfer to a bowl and refrigerate for at least 30 minutes before serving.

COCONUT CURRY SOUP

protein, healthy fats, cleansing power

This is another recipe inspired by Café Gratitude. When I lived in San Francisco I would frequent the original Café in the Mission district. Their coconut curry soup was my all-time favorite. This is my version of the soup.

Serves 4–6

What You'll Need
4 cups Coconut Milk (page 58)
1 ½ teaspoons grated fresh ginger
1 medium garlic clove, minced
2 tablespoons lemon or lime juice
¼ cup cold pressed organic olive oil
1 tablespoon coconut nectar
1 tablespoon Indian curry powder
½ small jalapeño pepper, minced
¼ to ½ teaspoon of sea salt
1 medium tomato, de-seeded and diced (for topping only)
1 ripe Hass avocado, pitted, small dice
Small handful cilantro, stem removed

Method
In a high-speed blender, combine the coconut milk, ginger, garlic, lemon juice, olive oil, coconut syrup, curry powder, jalapeño, and salt. Blend until smooth. Transfer to a serving bowl; add chopped tomato, avocado, and cilantro as a topping.

Kitchen Sink Salad

vitamin and mineral packed, fiber, protein

My parents made this recipe up in the 1970s at our farm in Missouri. They had a 100 percent self-sustaining farm and grew much of the food that we ate. This salad is a little bit of everything! They would put whatever they had in a bowl and make it a feast.

Serves 4

What You'll Need
4 cups fresh spinach, tightly packed
8 cups shredded kale, tightly packed
Lemon Tahini Dressing (page 128)
4 medium red radishes, thinly sliced
½ cup basil, minced
1 medium red bell pepper, cored and julienned
1 large ripe Hass avocado, pitted and diced
¼ cup fresh dill, minced
¼ cup fresh parsley, minced
¼ cup fresh mint, minced
½ cup raw organic pumpkin seeds
1 cup raw organic walnuts
1 medium cucumber, peeled and diced
3 medium carrots, diced or grated

Method
In a large bowl, combine the spinach, kale, and dressing. Toss to combine. Let the dressing marinate the greens while you prepare the remaining ingredients.

To the salad, add the radishes, basil, red bell pepper, avocado, dill, parsley, mint, pumpkin seeds, walnuts, cucumber, and carrots. Toss to combine. Serve at once.

Clean + Filling Salad

> vitamin and mineral packed, fiber, protein

I love this salad! I love how it looks; the heirloom carrots are absolutely beautiful. When you shave them with a vegetable peeler, it brings to focus the pure beauty of the food. The mint and dried cherries really make the flavors in this dish pop.

Serves 4

What You'll Need

1 large head romaine or butter lettuce, chopped
¼ watermelon radish, or 4 red radishes, sliced thin
5 heirloom carrots, peeled into strips
¼ cup goji berries
1 small green apple, cored and chopped
1 cup red cabbage, sliced thin using a mandoline
⅓ cup dried sour cherries or dried cranberries
⅓ cup fresh mint, minced
½ cup microgreens
Orange Vinaigrette (page 128)

Method

Wash and dry the chopped lettuce, and place into a large salad bowl. Layer on radish, carrot strips, goji berries, apple, cabbage, cherries, mint, and microgreens. Toss the entire salad in the dressing and serve.

EAT THE RAINBOW SALAD

| anti-cancer properties, boosts immunity, fiber filled |

This salad is full of life, minerals, vitamins, and high vibrations! There is something to be said about eating beautiful food. When you take the time to really bring beauty to the table, your body will feel it. It's so much more fun to eat gorgeous food! I like to decorate my salads with edible flowers that are in season; it adds a really lovely look to the salad. Eat your rainbow!

Serves 4

What You'll Need
1 large head romaine lettuce, chopped
2 cups shredded rainbow chard, packed tightly
Salad dressing of choice (page 126–128)
½ large cucumber, peeled and chopped
½ large yellow bell pepper, cored and diced
½ small head red cabbage, chopped
½ large red beet, julienned
3 medium red radishes, sliced thin on a mandoline
½ ripe Hass avocado, pitted, diced
½ ear of organic corn, taken off the cob
3 large carrots, cut into ¼-inch dice
⅓ cup fresh dill, minced
⅓ cup fresh parsley, minced
⅓ cup fresh fennel bulb, shaved
¼ cup raw organic raw sunflower seeds
¼ cup raw organic almonds
Edible flowers, optional garnish

Method
In a large bowl, massage the lettuce and chard with your favorite dressing. Add the cucumber, bell pepper, red cabbage, beet, radishes, avocado, corn, carrot, dill, parsley, fennel, sunflower seeds, and almonds. Toss together and garnish with flowers, if using. Serve at once.

SEDONA LOVE SALAD

fiber, antioxidants, healthy fats

I had to represent Sedona, Arizona in this book. What I love most about Sedona is the outstanding colors, how they are opposites (red and green, orange and blue) but somehow complement each other and create a marvelous beauty. This salad is one I made up when I was living in Sedona, and the colors in it represent the area perfectly.

Serves 4

What You'll Need
1 large head romaine lettuce, chopped
½ cup arugula
¼ cup baby chives, minced
1 ripe Hass avocado, pitted and diced
10 fresh blackberries, sliced
1 golden beet, grated
3 carrots, grated
5 dates, pitted and chopped
¼ cup hemp seeds
1 cup goji berries
1 cup dried mulberries
Orange Vinaigrette (page 128)

Method
In a large bowl, combine the chopped lettuce, arugula, chives, avocado, berries, beets, carrot, dates, hemp seeds, goji berries, and mulberries. Pour on the dressing and toss to combine. Serve with love.

MARINATED ASPARAGUS SALAD

protein rich, healthy fats, fiber

Asparagus is a vegetable that is naturally very high in protein. Two cups of asparagus have six grams of protein. That's really high for a green veggie! I used to make this salad for one of my private clients in Los Angeles, she loved it so much. It does call for the dehydrator so it's best to make this recipe when you have a little more time to spare; it's a really simple process that packs some serious flavor.

Serves 4

20 spears asparagus
2 tablespoons organic raw olive oil
2 tablespoons Nama Shoyu
2 tablespoons minced shallot
2 teaspoons coconut sugar or maple syrup
¼ teaspoon garlic powder
6 cups fresh mixed greens, packed tightly
5 small rainbow radishes, sliced thin on the mandoline
1 cup raw sprouted almonds, chopped
10 dates, pitted and chopped
Orange Vinaigrette (page 128)
1 ripe Hass avocado, pitted and sliced thin

Method

Cut the ends off of the asparagus and place in a large bowl or pie dish. Whisk together the olive oil, Nama Shoyu, shallot, coconut sugar, and garlic in a bowl. Pour the mixture over the asparagus and let marinate for ten to twenty minutes, turning occasionally. You can also let the asparagus marinate overnight for an even richer taste. Once they are done marinating, transfer to dehydrator sheets and dehydrate for 5–8 hours at 118 degrees. They should be moist and easy to bite into. (If you don't have a dehydrator, you can use an oven. Set temperature to 250–300 and bake on low for 30 minutes. This wont be raw, but it still will be incredibly healthy!)

For the salad, in a large bowl, combine the lettuce greens, radishes, almonds, and dates. Add the dressing and toss to combine. Arrange the avocado and asparagus on top of the salad mixture and serve immediately.

FERMENTED BEET SALAD

live probiotics, liver health, zinc

Fermented foods are a fabulous and tasty way to get live probiotics. They're easy to make and can be added as a side dish or topper to many dishes. You can make this recipe with beets, or with any of your favorite foods to pickle, just use the same technique. The process of pickling takes a couple days, but once it's done you have fermented veggies that will last for months in the refrigerator!

Serves 4

Fermented Beets
2½ cups beets, peeled, quartered, and sliced
¾ cup carrots, peeled, quartered, and thinly sliced
1 medium onion, peeled, quartered, and sliced
½ cup kale, shredded and stemmed
2 tablespoons sea salt
½ clove garlic, minced
1 cup filtered water
1 tablespoon raw agave (optional)
2 tablespoons caraway seeds

Salad
2 cups of the fermented beets
1 zucchini, spiralized
1 green apple, shredded
⅓ cup pumpkin seeds
1 tablespoon olive oil
1 teaspoon lemon juice
Microgreens for topping

Method

For the fermented beets
In a large bowl, mix the vegetables and transfer to a quart-size, wide mouth mason jar. Firmly press the vegetables and seeds into jar with your hand or a large spoon.

Mix the water with salt, caraway seeds, and agave if using, and then pour over the vegetables, adding water if needed. The top of the vegetables should be at least one inch below the top of the jar.

Seal tightly and keep at room temperature for about 3 days before transferring to cold storage. Be sure to leave that one-inch barrier, otherwise the contents can explode.

For the salad
In a bowl, mix the beets, zucchini, apple, and pumpkin seeds, toss with olive oil and lemon juice, and top with the microgreens.

Mango Mint Salad

fiber rich, vitamin C, minerals

This is a really interesting and flavor-filled salad, clearly not your run of the mill salad ingredients. Everything marinates together and the flavors are so refreshing. Jicama is a very low-calorie root vegetable, however it is very high in dietary fiber and full of antioxidants.

Serves 4

What You'll Need
4 cups ripe mango, peeled and diced
3 scallions, minced
1 cup jicama, diced
½ cup raw organic coconut flakes
2 sprigs fresh mint, minced
3 tablespoons raw organic olive oil
2 tablespoons lime juice
1 tablespoon honey
Sea salt to taste

Method
In a large bowl, combine the mango, scallions, jicama, coconut, and mint. Set aside. In a small bowl, mix olive oil, lime juice, honey, and salt, and mix well. Pour the dressing onto the salad mixture and toss. Serve immediately.

EARTHY CAESAR CHOPPED SALAD

fiber, antioxidants, filled with vitamins

When you start to move toward a plant-based raw diet, it's important to have lots of recipes to choose from so that you don't get bored. This is a hearty salad that fills you up and excites your taste buds. The dressing on page 126 is one of my all time favorites! I make it in bulk.

Serves 4

What You'll Need

1 head kale or romaine lettuce, chopped

½ cup Earthy Caesar Dressing (page 126)

8 to 12 red cherry tomatoes, sliced

½ medium cucumber, peeled and diced

1 cup raw organic walnuts

½ cup sunflower seeds

Method

In a large bowl, combine the greens and dressing; set aside. Add remaining ingredients, toss, and serve immediately.

RAW SLAW

healthy fats, magnesium, protein

This is a great side dish or even a main with some added greens!

Serves 4

What You'll Need

2 cups purple cabbage, shredded

1 small red bell pepper, cored and julienned

2 tablespoons organic raw cashew butter

1 tablespoon organic raw tahini

1½ tablespoons lemon juice

2 to 3 dates, pitted

Pinch sea salt

Method

Place the shredded cabbage and bell pepper in a large bowl and set aside. In a blender, combine remaining ingredients; process to blend. You may need to add a little water. Add to the vegetables and toss to combine. Let marinate for at least 20 minutes before serving.

BABY KALE AND CARAMELIZED ALMOND SALAD

fiber, antioxidants, filled with vitamins

Another favorite of mine. When I have time, I make the caramelized almonds and they really add a pop to this simple salad. The almonds store for a long time so when you have some free time, mix up a batch and stick them in the dehydrator for your future salads.

Serves 4

What You'll Need
1 cup raw organic almonds, soaked for 5 hours
4 medium dates, pitted
2 tablespoons organic cold-pressed olive oil
¼ shallot, minced
1 large bunch baby kale or spinach
½ cup Orange Vinaigrette (page 128)
8 to 10 red cherry tomatoes, sliced in half
¼ cup peeled and diced cucumber
½ cup chopped carrots
Sea salt to taste

Method
For caramelized almonds (optional for this recipe)
In a food processor or blender, combine the dates, olive oil, shallot, and salt, and process until smooth. In a bowl, combine the soaked almonds with the date mixture. Transfer to Teflex sheets and dehydrate for 8 hours or until a caramel-like consistency forms.

NOTE
You will need to do this the night before serving the salad. Otherwise, just use regular almonds for a quicker version of the recipe.

For Salad
In a large bowl, combine the greens and the dressing, massaging the dressing into the greens. Add the tomatoes, cucumber, carrots, and salt to taste. Add the almonds and serve immediately.

WATERCRESS AND FRESH FIG SALAD

vitamin A, vitamin K, protein

Watercress is an amazing nutritious green. It's known for its skin-healing properties; it is also high in iodine, phytochemicals, vitamin A, vitamin C, and vitamin K. It has many cancer-fighting compounds that help the body turn over cells quicker. I try to sneak it into my smoothies, but I also love it as a salad. Figs are a great source of fiber and they happen to clear the body of mucus buildup. Needless to say, this salad will be doing wonders for your body!

Serves 4

What You'll Need

2 cups tightly packed watercress, rinsed and patted dry, or arugula
2 cups fresh spring greens
Balsamic Dressing (page 127)
1 large ripe Hass avocado, pitted and thinly sliced
6 large fresh Turkish figs, thinly sliced
Sea salt and crushed black pepper, to taste
½ cup Creamy Ricotta (page 134)
1 cup Sweet and Spicy Pistachios (page 138)

Method

In a large bowl, combine the greens and balsamic dressing. Add the avocado, figs, and salt and pepper to taste. Toss to combine. To top, add 3 tablespoons of cashew ricotta on top, broken up into natural little pieces, and top with the sweet and spicy pistachios! Serve and enjoy.

Sesame Cabbage Salad

vitamin A, vitamin K, protein

This is a flavor-packed salad, it's creamy, and easy to eat. It's very decadent but also incredibly healthy. I love this as a side dish or even on top of a green salad.

Serves 4

What You'll Need

6 medium carrots, shredded
½ head large purple cabbage, shredded
1 ½ tablespoons apple cider vinegar
1 tablespoon lemon juice
2 to 3 tablespoons almond butter or cashew butter
1 to 2 large dates, pitted coarsely chopped
1 tablespoon toasted sesame oil
1 tablespoon Nama Shoyu
½ cup raw organic pistachios or favorite nut
1 teaspoon white or black sesame seeds

Method

In a large bowl, combine the shredded carrots and cabbage. Set aside.

In a high-speed blender, combine the vinegar, lemon juice, nut butter, dates, sesame oil, and Nama Shoyu. Pour the blended mixture onto the carrots and cabbage, toss, and let marinate for five minutes. Garnish with the pistachios and sesame seeds.

CUCUMBER AVOCADO CHOPPED

hydrating, skin saver, alkalizing

This is one of my all-time favorite summer salads. It's so refreshing but still fills you up. Simple, available ingredients that anyone can get at any time!

Serves 4

What You'll Need

2 large ripe Hass avocados, pitted

3 cups cucumber, peeled and small diced

2 medium green apples, sliced thin

2½ tablespoons fresh basil, minced

2 tablespoons lemon or lime juice

1 tablespoon apple cider vinegar

1 tablespoon coconut nectar or honey

2 tablespoons organic cold pressed olive oil

Sea salt and freshly ground black pepper

Method

Dice one avocado and slice the other into thin slices. Set the avocado slices aside and place the diced avocado in a large bowl. To the bowl, add the cucumber, apples, basil, lemon juice, vinegar, coconut nectar or honey, olive oil, and salt and pepper to taste. Toss to combine. The avocado should be chunky, not mushed; it's okay if it gets a bit creamy, but make sure to leave some dices whole. Let the mixture marinate for 5 minutes or so in the refrigerator.

To serve, place a large round cookie cutter or ring mold on a salad plate and spoon a portion of the salad mixture into it, pressing down to fill the mold. Repeat with the remaining salad. Depending on your mold size you should have enough for four salads. Place the sliced avocado around the top of each salad. Sprinkle with salt and pepper.

DRESSINGS, SAUCES & SIDES

For many, sauces and dressings make the dish, adding exciting textures and new interesting flavors! Sides and dips are great small meal options and can energize any salad or mundane meal. This section is full of fun recipes to help make your raw food experience be rich and enlivening. Once you learn the basics of dehydrating, you'll surely be whipping up your own raw food condiments and dressings.

A basic rule to remember when working with food and developing your own recipes is this: every recipe should have fat, sweet, acid, and salt in order for it to be well-rounded. Dressings are a great example of this. Easy example: Raspberry dressing. Raspberries (sweet), lemon (acid), olive oil (fat), garlic salt (salt). Using this rule, you can make quick and amazing recipes.

EARTHY CAESAR DRESSING

This is a creamy salad dressing that can be used on any salad, but it goes especially well with the chopped Caesar on page 117. I use dulse or nori, which is a raw seaweed that give it an anchovy flavor without the real fish.

Makes 2 cups

What You'll Need

½ cup raw organic cashews, soaked
⅓ cup pine nuts, dry
2 tablespoons organic cold-pressed olive oil
⅓ cup lemon juice
½ cup water
1 teaspoon nutritional yeast
2 small dates, pitted and coarsely chopped
3 large basil leaves, minced
1 large garlic clove, minced
¼ teaspoon cracked black pepper
2 teaspoons dulse or nori flakes
Sea salt to taste

Method

In a high-speed blender combine cashews, pine nuts, olive oil, lemon juice, water, nutritional yeast, dates, basil, garlic, pepper, and dulse. Blend until well combined, adding salt to taste. Store in a glass container with a tight-fitting lid. Keeps for seven days in refrigerator.

Classic Balsamic

This is my go-to dressing. You can "dress" it up a bit with your favorite spices and herbs! I like to keep mine super simple. This dressing makes all my salads taste amazing!

Makes 2 cups

What You'll Need

½ cup organic cold-pressed olive oil
½ cup apple cider vinegar
2 tablespoons raw honey
½ teaspoon powdered garlic

½ teaspoon dried parsley
¼ teaspoon black pepper
¼ teaspoon sea salt

Method

Simply combine oil, vinegar, honey, garlic, parsley, pepper, and salt in a small bowl, whisk with a fork, and enjoy on your favorite bed of greens.

Creamy Cilantro Avocado Dressing

This is a great dressing for kale salads. It's super creamy and coats the kale well. I also love using this dressing on kelp noodles!

Makes 2 cups

What You'll Need

1 medium avocado, pitted and coarsely
    chopped
¼ cup organic brown rice vinegar
½ cup organic cold-pressed olive oil
1 tablespoon nutritional yeast
1 small garlic clove, minced

½ cup cilantro, fresh
1 tablespoon green chives, minced
1 date, pitted
¼ tablespoon sea salt
¼ cup filtered water

Method

In a high-speed blender, combine the avocado, vinegar, oil, nutritional yeast, garlic, cilantro, chives, date, salt, and water, and blend until smooth; add water as needed for desired consistency. Store in a glass container with a tight-fitting lid where it will keep well for 3 days in the refrigerator.

ORANGE VINAIGRETTE

This is a sweet and sour style of dressing; the orange juice really gives it a unique flavor. I love this dressing on any style of Asian dish. It really makes flavors pop.

Makes 1 cup

What You'll Need

¼ cup organic cold pressed olive oil

¼ cup organic white wine vinegar

¼ cup fresh orange juice

2 tablespoons coconut nectar
  or coconut sugar

½ medium clove garlic, minced

Pinch sea salt

Black pepper to taste

Method

For a creamy dressing, combine all ingredients in a high-speed blender, and blend until well combined.

For a more traditional vinaigrette, whisk all the ingredients together in a large metal bowl until well combined. Store in a glass container with a tight-fitting lid. Keeps for five days in the refrigerator.

LEMON TAHINI DRESSING

This is my mom's favorite dressing. She is actually the original creator of this recipe. I've tweaked it a bit over the years, but this is a Charity original!

Makes 2 cups

What You'll Need

⅔ cup raw organic tahini

1 tablespoon organic light non-GMO
  miso paste

4 tablespoons lemon juice

3 tablespoons organic toasted sesame oil

½ cup olive oil

1 small garlic clove

½ cup filtered water as needed

1 tables spoon Nama Shoyu

Method

In a high-speed blender, combine all ingredients. Blend until well combined. Store in a glass container with a tight-fitting lid. This dressing will keep well for 5 days in refrigerator.

California Pesto

Pistachios are my favorite nut! Matthew Kenney, my former boss and forever inspirational chef, inspired this recipe. Matthew is an incredible plant-based celebrity chef—he has a similar pesto that is used in his Classic Lasagna. I loved it so much I could eat it by the spoonful. This is my version of a fresh, fragrant, delicious pesto.

Makes 2½ cups

What You'll Need

2 cups organic raw pistachios, dry
¼ cup organic raw pine nuts
2 cups basil, tightly packed
½ cup spinach, tightly packed
¾ cup organic cold pressed olive oil

Method

In a food processor, combine the pistachios, pine nuts, basil, and spinach. Process to mix until well blended. Slowly drizzle in the olive oil to make a smooth paste. Add more oil if desired.

Cover the top of the pesto with a thin layer of oil if you are going to store the pesto for later use. It will keep well for 5 days in the refrigerator.

Chive Cream Cheese

healthy fats, vitamin B12, protein

I love this cheese! I use as a dip, a dressing, and a filling for many of my impromptu raviolis. It's a wonderful simple cheese that you can make in a matter of minutes.

Makes 2 cups

What You'll Need

1½ cups raw organic cashews, soaked
¼ cup minced chives
1 tablespoon minced shallot
1 tablespoon nutritional yeast
1½ teaspoons apple cider vinegar or lemon juice
½ teaspoon salt
½ cup water as needed

Method

In a food processor, combine all ingredients. Process, adding a little water at a time, until you reach a smooth, creamy consistency. The mixture should be fairly thick so the less water needed to blend, the better. Store in a glass jar with a tight-fitting lid, and it will keep for 4 days in the refrigerator.

Classic Live Pesto

plant protein, healthy fat, iron

This is my version of a classic pesto. It's very easy to make and wonderful on a variety of dishes. I love pairing this pesto with the fermented cheese (page 137) and creating a lovely cheese plate.

Makes 1½ cups

What You'll Need

1 cup fresh basil, tightly packed
½ cup fresh spinach, tightly packed
1 cup organic raw pine nuts, dry
2 tablespoons organic cold-pressed olive oil
1 small garlic clove, crushed
Sea salt and ground black pepper, to taste

Method

In a food processor, combine the basil, spinach, pine nuts, oil, garlic, and salt and pepper to taste. Process until well blended and ground to a paste. Use as is, or transfer to a glass container with a tight-fitting lid. Cover the top of the pesto with a thin layer of oil if you are going to store the pesto for later use. It will keep well for 5 days in the refrigerator.

RAW HUMMUS

calcium, immune boost, healthy fiber

Many people are sensitive to chickpeas; they tend to be hard to digest. This recipe is made with zucchini instead. Still creamy and flavorful, but easy to digest! A great way to enjoy fresh veggies!

Makes 2½ cups

What You'll Need

2 medium zucchinis, peeled and diced
3 tablespoons organic raw tahini
1½ tablespoon organic cold-pressed olive oil
1 large garlic clove, minced
⅛ teaspoon cumin
⅛ teaspoon white pepper
1 teaspoon agave (optional)
¼ teaspoon sea salt
Paprika, for garnish

Method

In a food processor, combine the zucchini, tahini, olive oil, garlic, cumin, pepper, agave (if using), and salt, and process until smooth and creamy. Transfer the mixture to a bowl and sprinkle with paprika. Serve with your favorite cut veggies. If not using right away, cover tightly and refrigerate or transfer to a jar with a tight-fitting lid. It will keep for 4 days in the refrigerator.

CREAMY RICOTTA

This is a great easy cheese that can be used as a filling for ravioli, lasagna, or even just as a vegetable dip. I love using parsley and chives in mine to flavor it up a little bit!

Makes 2 cups

What You'll Need

I cup soaked raw organic macadamia nuts

½ cup soaked raw organic cashews

I tablespoon nutritional yeast

½ teaspoon garlic powder

I tablespoon minced parsley

½ teaspoon sea salt

¼ cup water, if needed

Method

In a food processor, combine all ingredients. Pulse to mix well, do not overblend—it should be a rough mix. Once the mixture is well combined, it is ready to use. If not using right away, transfer it to a glass jar with a tight-fitting lid where it will keep for 4 to 5 days in the refrigerator.

SUNFLOWER SOUR CREAM

vitamin E, anti-inflammatory, skin protection

This is a simple sauce that can be used in many Mexican-inspired dishes; it's also great on salads or as a vegetable dip.

Makes 1½ cups

What You'll Need

I cup soaked raw organic sunflower seeds

I tablespoon lemon juice

I tablespoon minced shallot

I teaspoon apple cider vinegar

½ teaspoon sea salt

¼ cup water

Method

In a high-speed blender, combine the sunflower seeds, lemon juice, shallot, vinegar, salt, and water. Blend until smooth. Add more water if needed. It should be a creamy mixture. Store in a glass container. Will keep for 4 days in the refrigerator.

CHEESY CHIPOTLE ALMONDS

vitamin b12, protein, healthy fat

These almonds are a great addition to a salad; they add a nice flavorful crunch. They are also wonderful snacks to have on hand!

Serves 8

What You'll Need
2 cups sprouted raw organic almonds
2 tablespoons organic maple syrup
1 tablespoon olive oil or coconut oil
1 tablespoon Nama Shoyu
2 tablespoons nutritional yeast
½ teaspoon ground chipotle spice
⅛ teaspoon cayenne
¼ teaspoon sea salt

Method
In a bowl, combine the almonds with maple syrup, oil, Nama Shoyu, nutritional yeast, ground chipotle, cayenne, and salt. Mix until well combined and the almonds are well coated. Spread the almonds on Teflex sheets and dehydrate at 115 degrees for 24 hours or until crisp.

FERMENTED CHEESE

probiotics, healthy fat, brain food

It's an amazing thing to be able to have cheese as a raw vegan! This cheese is so incredibly flavorful. If you were served this cheese at a restaurant I doubt you would know that it was vegan, let alone raw. I encourage you to try this and experiment with this recipe.

Makes 3 cups

What You'll Need

I cup cashews, soaked for I hour
I cup macadamia nuts, soaked for 2 hours
¼ cup water, as needed
I½ teaspoons probiotic powder
Flavor Options: Nutritional yeast, shallot, green onion, onion powder, turmeric (for color), beet juice (for color), chives, olives, cherries, nuts

Method

In a high-speed blender, combine the cashews, macadamias, and water, and blend until smooth. Be careful not to let the mixture heat up, as this will kill the live enzymes. Once you have a very creamy mixture, add the probiotic powder. Blend to incorporate. Pour the mixture into a double-layer cheesecloth or a nut milk bag and twist slightly to tighten. You don't want to strain it, just let a bit of the moisture come out. Set the mixture in a strainer, and put a weight on top of it (a book works great for this). It should ferment overnight. Do not let it ferment for over 48 hours. Once you have a slightly sour smell, you can flavor your cheese however you would like by combining the cheese mixture in a food processor with any of the suggested flavor options and processing until well mixed. To get a nice rind on the cheese, transfer the cheese to a ring mold or a round cookie cutter after adding the flavoring. Refrigerate overnight, then remove from the mold and dehydrate the cheese for 8 to 12 hours at 115 degrees.

SWEET & SALTY PISTACHIOS

B vitamins, eye health, heart health

One of my favorite snacks! I love sweet and salty treats; this one does the trick and gives me essential nutrients that my body can use!

Serves 8

What You'll Need

2 cups raw pistachios
2 tablespoons organic maple syrup
¼ cup olive oil
1 teaspoon nutritional yeast
¼ teaspoon salt or Nama Shoyu

Method

Mix pistachios, maple syrup, olive oil, yeast, and salt in a bowl and toss until pistachios are well covered. Place on Teflex sheets and dehydrate at 115 degrees for 24 hours or until crisp.

LIME IN THE COCONUT

I first had this when I was on vacation in Careyes, Mexico. The locals made something like this and it was so tasty! I've made it often since then for a quick and filling snack.

Serves 6

What You'll Need

4 cups young coconuts, flesh cut in strips
4 tablespoons lime juice
¼ teaspoon sea salt
½ teaspoon chili powder

Method

Cut the coconut into long strips and place in a shallow bowl. Add the lime juice and salt. Let marinate for 15 minutes. Lightly dust with chili powder and serve.

CLASSIC CHEESY KALE CHIPS

Everyone should learn how to make kale chips—even if you're not a raw foodist, these tasty treats are a far better choice for a crispy snack than overly processed potato chips and conventional snack foods. NOTE: If you don't own a dehydrator, you can bake the chips. Although they won't technically be raw, they still are a healthy snack alternative. Bake at the lowest available temperature on your oven.

Serves 6

What You'll Need

6 large bunches kale (40 to 60 leaves), well washed and spun dry
2 cups soaked raw organic macadamia nuts or cashews
¾ cup nutritional yeast
1 large garlic clove, minced
1 large red bell pepper, cored and coarsely chopped
2 tablespoons apple cider vinegar
2 tablespoons coconut sugar
½ large shallot, minced
1 teaspoon smoked paprika powder
½ teaspoon chipotle powder
Pinch sea salt

Method

Remove the stems from the kale leaves. Tear the leaves into large pieces and set aside.

In a food processor, combine the nuts, yeast, garlic, and bell pepper and process until smooth. Slowly add the vinegar, coconut sugar, shallot, paprika, chipotle, and salt, and blend until smooth. Massage the seasoning mixture into the kale pieces. Use your hands to make sure all of the leaves are covered. Dehydrate at 115 degrees for at least 15 hours. The chips should be crispy. Store in a plastic ziplock in a cool dry place. Keeps for 2 weeks to 2 months depending on the climate.

Pumpkin Seed Butter

vitamin E, skin saver, red blood cell function

When I was pregnant I was eating this butter by the tablespoon! I couldn't get enough. The reason why? Pumpkin seeds are loaded with zinc, folic acid, and vitamin B. My body and baby were leading me to the foods I needed and this one happened to have a lot of crucial nutrients.

8 Servings

What You'll Need

4 cups sprouted and dehydrated pumpkin seeds
1 tablespoon pumpkin seed oil (if needed)
½ teaspoon sea salt

Method

In a food processor, combine the pumpkin seeds, oil, and salt, until well blended. This may take several minutes. You might find you need a bit more oil, but just take your time and let it process. The less oil, the better it tastes!

Almond Butter

protein, healthy lipid levels, fiber

Almond butter continues to go up in price—the last time I went to buy some it was nearly thirty dollars! That's absolutely outrageous, and you can make your own for a fraction of the price. Here is how.

8 Servings

What You'll Need

2 cups sprouted and dehydrated almonds
1 tablespoon organic raw almond oil (if needed)
½ teaspoon sea salt

Method

In a food processor, combine the almonds, oil, and salt. Process until well blended. Continue to process for several minutes until a smooth creamy butter forms.

Spicy Pico de Gallo

This recipe goes really well in salads, as a side, mixed in with guacamole, and on the Hearty Raw Tacos (page 171). It's fresh, light, and packed with flavor.

Makes 2 cups

What You'll Need
2 cups coarsely chopped cherry tomatoes
½ small jalapeño, minced
2 tablespoons minced cilantro
2 tablespoons chopped red onion
Pinch sea salt
1 large lime, juiced

Method
In a bowl, combine the tomatoes, jalapeño, cilantro, onion, and salt. Toss to combine, and then cover with a lid or plastic wrap. Let marinate for at least 25 minutes before serving. Right before serving, add the lime juice and stir to combine. Store in a glass container with a tight-fitting lid. It will keep well for 5 days in the refrigerator.

COCONUT JERKY

healthy fats, protein, high fiber

This recipe is such an indulgence for me. I absolutely love it. It's a great snack or salad topper. My family is always munching on this.

Serves 4

What You'll Need

5 cups coconut flakes (large, not shredded)
¼ cup Nama Shoyu
2 teaspoons apple cider vinegar
1 small clove garlic, minced
1 tablespoon shallot, minced
¼ cup maple syrup or coconut sugar
1 cup olive oil
¼ teaspoon turmeric
1½ teaspoons ground cumin
1 teaspoon cumin seeds

Method

Put coconut flakes into a bowl and set aside. In a second bowl, combine the Nama Shoyu, vinegar, garlic, shallot, maple syrup, olive oil, turmeric, cumin powder, and cumin seed. Add the sauce to the coconut meat, and let marinate for 45 minutes to an hour. Spread the coconut on the dehydrator sheets and dehydrate at 115 degrees for five hours or until crisp. This yummy snack and topping will last roughly one month when sealed and kept dry.

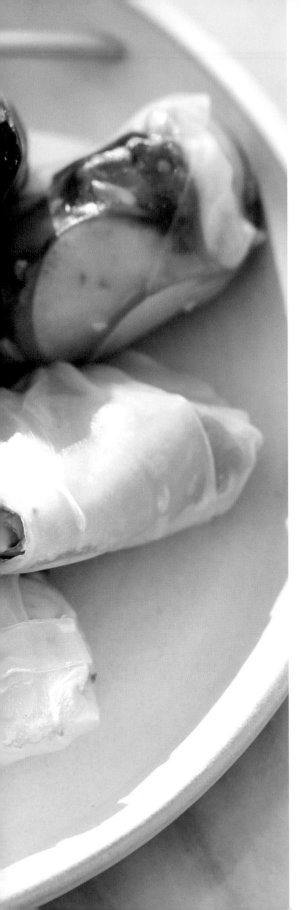

MAIN DISHES

My main focus when writing *Raw and Radiant* was to provide people with healthy raw meals that didn't take days to make. There is a time and a place for raw gourmet cuisine. I enjoy making beautiful, well-thought-out meals for my friends and family when I have the time, but in my daily life, I'm busy. In addition to my work, I have a husband, an extremely active four-year-old, and a life that I love to spend time on. If I were to make gourmet meals every day, I wouldn't be able to spend my time on these joys of life, because I would always be preparing food.

I put my favorite quick meals in this book so that you too can enjoy the benefits of raw food without losing your social life! I want you to be healthy and enjoy your life. These are incredibly tasty and fairly basic meals that will sustain you and even impress your non-raw friends and family. Thankfully, raw food is becoming more mainstream and you can find healthy raw cuisine in many cities. I love dining at my favorite raw restaurants and enjoy the beautiful and interesting menus. It's also become easier to find already pre-pared raw snacks to keep you going through the day.

Maple and Sage Infused Sweet Potato Ravioli

blood sugar balancing, iron, sulphur

This is a great Fall dish. I love when the weather starts to change and the farmers markets start carrying winter squash and sweet potatoes. This dish can easily be made with butternut squash or yams. You can also substitute the sage for another favorite herb that is in season.

Serves 4

What You'll Need

2 large sweet potatoes, peeled
¼ teaspoon sea salt
¼ cup plus 1 tablespoon olive oil, divided
1 tablespoon minced fresh sage, or favorite herb
1 tablespoon minced green chives
1 tablespoon maple syrup
1 tablespoon apple cider vinegar
1 teaspoon Dijon mustard
1½ cups raw organic cashews, soaked for 1 hour
1½ tablespoons nutritional yeast
1 teaspoon minced fresh parsley
1 teaspoon minced shallot
¼ cup water, as needed
¼ teaspoon sea salt

Method

Cut the sweet potatoes into thin slices using a mandolin or sharp knife. Arrange the slices on parchment paper, sprinkle with salt and 1 tablespoon of the olive oil, and set aside.

In a blender add the remaining ¼ cup olive oil, sage, chives, maple syrup, vinegar, and mustard. Blend on high, adding water if you prefer a thinner dressing. Set aside.

In a food processor, combine the cashews, nutritional yeast, parsley, shallot, water, and ¼ teaspoon salt. Process until smooth.

To assemble, one by one, place a slice of sweet potato on a cutting board or parchment paper and spoon 1 tablespoon of cashew filling in the center and top with a dollop of the maple sage dressing. Repeat with the remaining ingredients. To make a traditional ravioli, top with another layer or leave open face. Arrange on a plate and serve.

LOVELY MISO KELP NOODLES

fiber filled, thyroid health, iron

Kelp noodles are a great alternative to wheat and rice noodles. They're super quick to make and they are almost calorie free. For someone wanting to lose weight yet still feel full, they are my first suggestion. I love changing up the sauce I use on them, though this recipe is my all-time favorite. If you can't find kelp noodles, this dish can be made with two yellow squashes spiralized.

Serves 4

What You'll Need
1 tablespoon organic GMO free miso
1½ tablespoons organic raw almond butter
1 teaspoon apple cider vinegar
1 tablespoon Nama Shoyu
1 (1-inch) piece ginger, grated
2 teaspoons organic toasted sesame oil
¼ cup water
1 tablespoon coconut nectar
1 (16-ounce) bag raw kelp noodles, well rinsed
1 cup fresh spinach, tightly packed
1 medium heirloom carrot, peeled into strips
¼ cucumber, peeled and coarsely chopped
½ cup crushed almonds

Method
In a high-speed blender, combine the miso, almond butter, apple cider vinegar, Nama Shoyu, ginger, sesame oil, water, and coconut nectar. Blend well.

Place the rinsed kelp noodles in a bowl and add the sauce. Let marinate for at least an hour or overnight (the longer the better). To serve, combine the marinated noodles with the spinach, carrots, cucumber, and almonds. Toss to combine and serve.

Coconut Curry Bowl

warming, fiber rich, blood cleansing

As a raw foodist, the winter can be a very trying time. This is a great dish to eat during the colder months; it's warming from the inside out. The spices in this recipe are also very healing; I love incorporating them into my dishes as often as possible.

Serves 4

What You'll Need
2 medium yellow squash
1 cup shredded kale or spinach, tightly packed
2 tablespoons coconut oil
1 cup soaked cashews or young coconut flesh
¼ cup raw organic sunflower seeds
½ teaspoon curry powder
¼ teaspoon turmeric
⅛ teaspoon cinnamon
1 teaspoon onion powder
1 tablespoon coconut sugar
2 tablespoons white wine vinegar
Pinch of salt
⅓ cup Coconut Jerky (page 143)
3 leaves basil, chopped
¼ cup pistachios or favorite nut
Microgreens for topping

Method
Spiralize the yellow squash and transfer to a bowl. Add the shredded kale and set aside.

In a food processor, combine the coconut oil, cashews or coconut flesh, sunflower seeds, curry powder, turmeric, cinnamon, onion powder, coconut sugar, vinegar, and salt. Process into a creamy sauce. Pour the sauce onto the kale and the noodles. Massage it into the kale and noodles to make sure the flavors are incorporated. Top with Coconut Jerky, chopped basil, crushed pistachios, and microgreens.

RUSTIC FLAT BREAD PIZZA

full of fiber, healthy fats, lycopene

One of the most versatile recipes there is! You can customize this recipe to fit your vegetables and herbs. You can even play with the sauce by adding red wine or spice! There is a lot of room for creativity here.

Serves 6–8

What You'll Need

For the Crust:
½ cup medium sweet white onion, chopped
3 tablespoons raw organic olive oil
1 medium yellow squash, coarsely chopped
1½ cup raw organic walnuts
1 date, pitted
¼ to ½ teaspoon sea salt
¼ cup ground golden flax

For the Sauce:
2 medium Roma tomatoes, coarsely chopped
½ cup soaked sun-dried tomatoes
1 tablespoon organic cold-pressed olive oil
1 teaspoon minced fresh oregano
Sea salt to taste

Choice of Toppings:
1 tablespoon capers
5 to 8 Kalamata olives, pitted and thinly sliced
½ red bell pepper, cored and julienned
1 cup fresh arugula
1 onion, sliced and dehydrated
¼ cup chopped fresh broccoli
2 raw organic macadamia nuts, grated
1 cup dehydrated red onions

Method for Crust

Use a mandolin, if you have one, or a sharp knife, to thinly slice one of the onions, and set aside. Coarsely chop the remaining onion and transfer to a food processor. Add the olive oil, squash, walnuts, dates, and salt. Blend until smooth, add the sliced onions, and pulse a few times. Transfer to a bowl, stir in the ground flax seeds, and set aside to thicken, about 5 minutes.

Spread the mixture onto Teflex sheets, about ¼- to ½-inch thick, then cut into desired shapes and dehydrate for 12 to 24 hours. *You may want to turn them after 8 hours.

Method for Sauce

In a food processor, combine the raw and sun-dried tomatoes, olive oil, oregano, and sea salt. Process for about 30 seconds, or until desired consistency is reached (smooth or a bit chunky).

To Assemble:

Put your crust on a nice serving platter or a cutting board, spread your pizza sauce on and any other sauces (such as pesto), and top with your favorite toppings. Serve immediately.

PROTEIN + VEGETABLE MEDLEY

antioxidants, omegas, heavy metal detoxifier

It gets so hot in Sedona during the summer. Simple salads are my staple meals throughout the summer. This salad ensures a full serving of protein and packs a lot of flavor. I always suggest this kind of salad to my clients when they are detoxing. You get a salad that tastes great, but detoxes you at the same time.

Serves 4

What You'll Need

2 medium cucumbers, peeled and diced
1 medium green apple, cored and diced
2 medium ripe Hass avocado, pitted and diced
2 teaspoons coconut nectar
3 to 4 tablespoons lemon juice
1 small garlic clove, minced
8 tablespoons hemp seeds
Small bunch cilantro, coarsely chopped
16 walnuts, chopped
½ cup pomegranate seeds
¼ teaspoon sea salt

Method

In a bowl, combine the cucumber, apple, avocado, coconut nectar, and lemon juice. Add the garlic, hemp seeds, cilantro, walnuts, pomegranate seeds, and salt. Toss together until well combined. Serve immediately.

MEDITERRANEAN VEGGIE PASTA

vitamin A, protein, fiber rich

Healthy, full of flavor, and quick to make. This is a great blend between a salad and pasta. The textures and flavors work really well together.

Serves 4

What You'll Need

1 cup yellow cherry tomatoes, coarsely chopped

¾ cup organic raw walnuts

2 tablespoons pine nuts, dry

2 tablespoons organic cold-pressed olive oil, plus more for lettuce

1 teaspoon red wine vinegar

¾ cup water (if needed)

2 small zucchini or yellow squash

⅓ cup pitted Kalamata olives, cut in half

Sea salt and ground black pepper, to taste

1 medium head butter lettuce, chopped

Method

In a blender, combine the tomatoes, walnuts, pine nuts, 1 tablespoon of the olive oil, red wine vinegar, and sea salt. Blend until smooth, adding water as needed. Set aside.

Use a spiralizer to spiralize the zucchini, or cut it into long strips using a julienne peeler. Transfer the zucchini to a large bowl. Add the remaining 1 tablespoon olive oil, Kalamata olives, a pinch of salt and black pepper to taste. Add the reserved sauce and toss to combine.

Place the lettuce in a separate bowl and drizzle on a small amount of olive oil and season with salt to taste. To serve, divide the lettuce amount serving bowls or plates and top with the noodles.

RAINBOW RICE ROLLS

sulphur, vitamin A, calcium

This is my go-to meal when I'm in a hurry. I throw it together and I'm never disappointed. It tastes great and it's done in five minutes. Raw on the go! Instead of using Nama Shoyu, you can add a bit of your favorite salad dressing.

Makes 4 rice rolls

What You'll Need

4 rice sheets (found in the Asian foods section of the grocery store)
½ red beet, shredded
¼ cup kimchi or sauerkraut (optional)
½ red bell pepper, cored and julienned
1 carrot, sliced thin
1 medium ripe Hass avocado, pitted and sliced
Nama Shoyu or Tahini Dressing (page 128) for dipping

Method

Prepare a large 3-inch deep pan with room temperature water. Lay a dry rice paper in the water for 5–10 seconds. Take out, and lay on a flat surface such as a cutting board. Wipe with a paper towel to take away excess moisture.

Spread ¼ of the almond butter on the rice paper center. Add a little beet, kimchi, bell pepper, carrot, and avocado, making sure to leave enough ingredients for your next 3 rolls.

Fold the sides over and then roll like a burrito.

Place on a plate and repeat.

CUCUMBER AND HEMP SEED TABBOULEH

protein, aids digestion, lycopene

A great summertime dish, refreshing and full of health promoting properties. This is a very easy and quick meal. I make it when I'm in a rush and need to fuel my body quickly.

Serves 4

1 cup chopped parsley
1 cucumber, peeled, seeded, and finely diced
1 cup cherry tomatoes, chopped
¾ cup hemp seeds
2 tablespoons green onions, minced
¼ cup chopped mint leaves
6 tablespoons lemon juice
1 tablespoon sunflower butter
1 small clove garlic, minced
1 teaspoon sea salt

Method

In a bowl, combine the parsley, cucumber, tomato, hemp seeds, green onions, and mint leaves, and toss to combine. Add the lemon juice, sunflower butter, garlic, and salt. If the sunflower butter is too thick, add a bit of water before mixing. Toss until well combined. Let marinate for ten to fifteen minutes, and then serve.

SAVORY CREPES WITH OYSTER MUSHROOMS

healthy fats, protein, good fiber

This is one of my longer recipes, but it is worth it. Such a yummy, savory treat. When I'm really wanting something cooked, this is what I opt for. It's very impressive to many non-raw foodists. A great holiday food option!

Serves 4

What You'll Need

Crepes

3 medium zucchinis, pureed (about four cups after pureeing in your blender)

1 medium shallot, minced

¾ cup flax seeds

½ cup coconut meat

2 tablespoons organic cold-pressed olive oil

1 tablespoon Herbs de Provence

Filling

2 cups oyster mushrooms, tightly packed

4 tablespoons organic cold-pressed olive oil, divided

Pinch of salt

1 cup cashews, soaked

½ cup pine nuts, dry

1½ tablespoons lemon juice

1 tablespoon minced parsley

1 tablespoon minced chives

Chopped fresh herbs, optional garnish

Method

Crepes: In a food processor, combine the zucchini, shallot, flax seeds, coconut meat, oil, and herbs. Blend until smooth. Transfer the mixture onto Teflex sheets in 3-inch rounds, about ¼-inch thick—it should make 8 crepes. Dehydrate at 115 degrees for 8 to 12 hours. The crepes should be dried enough that you can peel them off of the Teflex without them ripping. They should be easy to handle. If not, you might need more dehydration time depending on your climate. Once they are done, set aside and make the filling.

Filling: Chop the oyster mushrooms and place in a bowl with 2 tablespoons olive oil and a pinch of salt. Let them sit for about 20 minutes while you make the cream.

In a food processor, combine the cashews, pine nuts, lemon juice, parsley, chives, and salt and pepper to taste. Blend till creamy. Add the mushrooms and pulse lightly to combine. Do not over process.

To assemble, arrange the crepes on a flat work surface, one at a time, and spoon some of the mushroom mixture into the crepe, roll up, and arrange on a plate. Repeat with the remaining ingredients. Spoon any remaining sauce over the top of the crepes. Sprinkle with fresh herbs, if using.

Classic Raw Lasagna

> full of fiber, healthy fats, lycopene

This is a classic raw food staple; every raw food chef has a version of this recipe. Once you have the components made, this is a super quick recipe! I often make the cheese and sauce ahead of time so that I can throw this meal together in minimal time.

Serve 2–4

What You'll Need

Lasagna
2 large zucchini, sliced thin with
    a mandoline or sharp knife
1 tablespoon olive oil
Sea salt
1 cup California Pesto (page 129)
1 cup Creamy Ricotta (page 134)
1 cup Marinara
¼ cup raw black olives, pitted and sliced
1 small bunch fresh basil, for layering

Marinara
24 oz. sun-dried tomatoes
    (soaked or in oil)
1 large tomato, seeded and chopped
2 pitted dates
½ teaspoon onion powder
1 teaspoon apple cider vinegar
1½ teaspoon olive oil
¼ teaspoon salt

Method

Lasagna: Brush the zucchini slices with the olive oil. Add a bit of sea salt to tenderize. Set aside for fifteen minutes while you prepare the remaining components.

Arrange a layer of the zucchini slices in the bottom of a shallow baking dish. Top with a layer of the pesto, followed by a layer of ricotta, marinara, olives, and basil. Repeat with the remaining ingredients ending with a layer of the marinara garnished with olives or basil.

Marinara: If you are using sun-dried tomatoes in oil, drain the oil. If you are using soaked ones, drain the water. Combine sun-dried tomatoes, fresh chopped tomato, dates, onion powder, vinegar, olive oil, and salt, in your food processor. Blend until well-combined.

RAW VEGAN SUSHI

iodine, vitamin E, fiber

This is a favorite meal of mine. I make it with cooked brown rice when I'm not wanting raw. It's a super beautiful way to impress guests and enjoy a unique meal. The tahini dipping sauce makes it insanely good!

Serves 4–8

What You'll Need

Sushi

A sushi rolling mat

5 roasted nori seaweed sheets

1 cup chopped jicama or cauliflower

½ cup pine nuts, dry

½ teaspoon salt

1 tablespoon raw organic almond butter

1 tablespoon toasted sesame oil (optional)

½ tablespoon maple syrup

1 medium carrot, julienned

½ cup red beet, shredded

1 medium ripe Hass avocado, pitted and thinly sliced

Tahini Dipping Sauce

¼ cup tahini

1 tablespoon brown rice miso

1 tablespoon lemon juice

1 tablespoon toasted sesame oil

1 tablespoon coconut aminos or Nama Shoyu

1 clove garlic, minced

⅓ cup olive oil

pinch of salt

Method

To make the "rice" in a food processor, blend the jicama and pulse until rice texture. Strain out the liquid with a nut milk bag and then return to the food processor and add the pine nuts and sea salt. Pulse until a pulp forms. Set aside.

In a bowl combine the chopped nuts, almond butter, toasted sesame, maple syrup, and a pinch of salt.

Arrange a sheet of nori on a sushi mat; spread one-quarter of the jicama "rice" evenly on ¾ of the nori sheet. Arrange slices of carrot, beets, and avocado in a line near the bottom edge of the nori (closest to you). Spread the nut blend in a line. Roll up the sushi roll, using the sushi mat to roll it up tightly. Cut horizontally into six pieces. Repeat with the remaining ingredients. Arrange the sushi pieces on a platter.

For the dipping sauce combine tahini, miso, lemon juice, sesame oil, shoyu, garlic, olive oil, and salt in a high powered blender. Add a little water if you need it for blending.

Serve immediately and enjoy thoroughly!

SUMMER SQUASH PASTA + DANDELION GREEN PESTO

iron, protein, and fiber rich

This is an incredible recipe for liver and kidney health and can actually be cooked or raw. I If you don't own a spiralizer, you can use a mandoline to slice the squash. It should be very thin and delicate. If you aren't a big fan of bitters, you can replace the dandelion greens with spinach.

Serves 4

What You'll Need

3 large yellow squash or zucchini
I cup dandelion greens
2 cups basil, chopped
½ cup pine nuts, dry
I tablespoon hemp seeds
I teaspoon minced shallot
¼ cup olive oil
½ teaspoon sea salt
½ teaspoon ground black pepper
I tablespoon nutritional yeast (optional)

Method

Spiralize the squash or use a mandoline to slice, and transfer to a large bowl. Set aside in the refrigerator.

In a food processor combine the dandelion, basil, pine nuts, hemp seeds, shallot, olive oil, salt, pepper, and nutritional yeast. Process until a nice consistency forms.

Transfer the pesto to the noodles and toss with a fork. To assemble, just place on your favorite plate and enjoy!

*If you want to make this a heated meal, just toss in a skillet and cook with a little extra olive oil.

Golden Beet Ravioli

iron, healthy fats, brain power

This is another one of my recipes from my final at Matthew Kenney Culinary. I wanted to make something that my family members would really enjoy, that was elegant but still comforting. I ended up loving this recipe so much that I had to sneak it into the book!

Serves 4

What You'll Need

2 to 3 large golden beets
¼ cup organic cold-pressed olive oil, divided
Sea salt
1 large Portobello mushroom, stemmed and chopped
1½ cups raw organic walnuts
2 tablespoons Nama Shoyu or coconut aminos
1 tablespoon apple cider vinegar or lemon juice
3 tablespoons nutritional yeast
½ teaspoon truffle oil (optional)
2 tablespoons olive oil
2 cups Creamy Ricotta (page 134)

Method

Slice the beets very thin on a mandoline (or with a sharp knife), then brush the beet slices with 1 tablespoon of the olive oil and sprinkle with salt to taste. Set aside to let them soften while preparing the filling.

In a food processor, combine the mushrooms and walnuts, pulse to chop, then add the remaining olive oil, shoyu, vinegar, nutritional yeast, truffle oil (if using), olive oil, and salt to taste. Be careful not to overprocess, this should be a textured mixture.

Arrange half of the beet slices on a cutting board or parchment paper. Spoon 1 tablespoon of mushroom filling onto the center of each beet slice and top with 1 tablespoon of the ricotta. Top with the remaining beet slices and press the sides together. You can also leave the ravioli un-pressed (as pictured).

Simple Tostada

This recipe is easy and really tasty. If you want to make a quicker version you can just omit the tostada shell and use collard greens or romaine lettuce. I make the tostada shells ahead of time and store them in the refrigerator until I'm ready to use them.

Serves 6

What You'll Need
For the tortilla
2½ cups fresh corn kernels
1¼ cups chopped red bell pepper
½ cup water
1-2 tablespoons fresh lime juice
1½ teaspoons chili powder
1½ teaspoons cumin
1 teaspoon sea salt
¾ cup ground flax seeds

Toppings
Sunflower Sour Cream (page 134)
1 cup shredded red cabbage
1 cup shredded romaine lettuce
Spicy Pico de Gallo (page 141)
½ large ripe Hass avocado, pitted and diced

Method
In a food processor combine the corn, bell pepper, water, lime juice, chili powder, cumin, and salt, and process to blend. Pour the mixture into a bowl and stir in the ground flax seed. Let the mixture set for 10 minutes to thicken. Spread the mixture onto dehydrator sheets in 3-inch circles—this makes around 12 to 14 shells. Dehydrate for 8 to 15 hours at 115 degrees until crunchy or you can leave them a bit soft for a soft style taco. To serve, top the dehydrated tortillas with your choice of the suggested toppings.

RAW PAD THAI

protein, skin saver, fiber

Pad Thai is one of my favorite cooked Thai dishes, but it's often loaded with sugar. This is a super clean version that packs all the flavor but not the sugar high.

Note: toasted sesame oil is technically not raw, but I sometimes use it as a flavoring.

Serve 4

What You'll Need
½ cup water
¾ cup raw almond butter
2 tablespoons toasted sesame oil
1½ tablespoons Nama Shoyu
1 small Thai red pepper, coarsely chopped
2 tablespoons lime juice
1½ tablespoons agave
1 small garlic clove, minced
2 large yellow squash
½ cup mung bean sprouts
10 sugar snap peas, trimmed and bias cut
½ cup soaked dehydrated almonds, finely chopped
12 cilantro leaves

Method
In a food processor, blend the water, almond butter, sesame oil, Nama Shoyu, Thai pepper, lime juice, agave, and garlic. Pulse until well combined. Set aside.

Use a spiralizer to spiralize the squash or use a julienne peeler to cut the squash into thin strips. Transfer the squash "noodles" to a large bowl. Pour in reserved almond sauce and let marinate for 5 minutes.

Once the squash is done marinating, add the bean sprouts, snap peas, almonds, and cilantro leaves. Mix together to combine and serve.

Mock Tuna Salad

fiber filled, healthy fats, calcium

This was another favorite of mine when I first went raw. I would sometimes put it on sprouted bread when I was in the transition phase.

Serves 4

What You'll Need
1 cup almonds, soaked
½ medium red onion, diced
2 tablespoons dulse flakes
¼ cup fresh dill, minced
3 large celery stalks, diced
Sea salt to taste
4 romaine lettuce leaves
Lemon-Tahini Dressing (page 128)

Method
Blend the almonds in a food processor until they are coarsely ground, but still chunky. Add the onion, dulse, dill, celery, and salt to taste. Process to combine, but do not over process.

To serve, scoop the mixture onto lettuce leaves and drizzle with the Lemon Tahini Dressing.

FETTUCCINE ALFREDO

healthy fats, omegas, fiber

This is a great dish for someone who is transitioning to a raw food diet; the cravings for pastas, cheese, and comfort foods can be strong. The texture of the zucchini and the creaminess of the nuts are perfect to replace the dairy- and carb-filled original. This dish is really nice on its own or with cherry tomatoes, basil, sage, dehydrated onions, olives, and a few pine nuts on top. You can play with your toppings.

Serves 4

What You'll Need
2 large zucchini
⅓ cup raw organic pine nuts, dry
¾ cup raw organic cashews, soaked
¼ cup raw organic macadamia nuts
½ small garlic clove, minced
2 teaspoons nutritional yeast
1 date, pitted and coarsely chopped
2 teaspoons lemon juice
1 teaspoon white wine vinegar
2 tablespoons olive oil
½ cup filtered water
½ teaspoon sea salt

Method
Peel and spiralize the zucchini or cut them into thin strips using a peeler, and transfer to a large bowl. Set aside.

In a food processor, combine the pine nuts, cashews, macadamia nuts, garlic, nutritional yeast, date, lemon juice, vinegar, olive oil, water, and salt. Blend the mixture, adding water as needed. This sauce should be creamy enough to hold to the noodles, but thin enough to mix easily with them.

Once the sauce is ready, add a bit of salt to the zucchini noodles and toss. Then pour the sauce over the noodles and combine.

Hearty Raw Tacos

vitamin C, healthy fats, heavy metal cleansing

Hearty is the key word here, these are really filling while not weighing you down. We love taco Tuesday at our house, and these get made often! I love setting up all the ingredients on the table so that everyone can pick out their favorite toppings.

Serves 4

What You'll Need
4 large purple cabbage or Swiss chard leaves
Chive Cream Cheese (page 129)
1 medium ripe Hass avocado, sliced
1 cup sliced red cherry tomatoes
½ cup shredded romaine lettuce
⅓ cup minced cilantro leaves
Spicy Pico de Gallo (page 141)

Method
Place the cabbage or Swiss chard leaves on a flat work surface and top each with a layer of chive cream cheese, avocado, tomatoes, lettuce, cilantro, and Pico de Gallo. Fold the leaves over and serve immediately. To help the tacos stay in place for presentation, you can use a toothpick to hold them in place.

SWEET TREATS

I got my start as a raw food chef working at a small restaurant preparing desserts and smoothies. I was overjoyed that I could enjoy desserts without the guilt and sluggishness I felt from standard desserts. Although I always practice moderation, I love indulging in fresh, healthy, raw desserts. This section is very special to me. I've spent years coming up with these recipes and hope that you and your family will enjoy them!

PERFECT PIE CRUST

This is my favorite go-to pie crust recipe. Simple and tasty. To use it as a savory crust, just remove the raisins and vanilla. You can replace them with shredded carrot or another kind of nut or seed. This can also be made with different nuts, such as raw organic walnuts, raw organic almonds, Brazil nuts, and raw organic pecans. It can also be made with dates, figs, or regular raisins. It just depends on the taste and density you are going for! Play with it, find your favorite. There are endless options.

Makes one 9-inch pie crust

What You'll Need
¼ cup raw organic coconut oil, plus more to oil pan
1½ cups raw organic macadamia nuts, dry
1 cup golden raisins
1 teaspoon vanilla extract
¼ teaspoon sea salt

Method
Lightly oil a 9-inch pie pan with coconut oil and set aside.

In a food processor, combine the macadamia nuts, raisins, vanilla, salt, and the ¼ cup coconut oil. Blend until well mixed and a dough-like consistency forms. Press the mixture into the prepared pan. Place in refrigerator to set until ready to use. If covered with plastic wrap, the crust will last for 3 months in the freezer.

Macaroons

In Scottsdale, Arizona, there used to be a little café called chakra 4. It was my favorite cafe! All organic, vegan, and tasty. Sadly, they closed recently . . . but I still make a version of one of my favorite treats from the café—the macaroons. I hope you enjoy them as much as I do.

Serve 8

What You'll Need
2 cups organic shredded coconut

1½ tablespoons powdered maca root

⅓ cup plus 1 tablespoon maple syrup

2 tablespoons vanilla extract

¼ teaspoon sea salt

½ cup coconut oil

Method
In a food processor, combine the shredded coconut, maca, maple syrup, vanilla, salt, and coconut oil. Process until a dough forms. Let the dough cool for a bit and then shape it into 1-inch balls. Arrange on a plate and chill for 20 minutes before serving. These store well in a glass jar with a tight-fitting lid in the refrigerator.

Irish Moss Paste

Irish moss is a great thickener for raw foods. It is a seaweed that gelatinizes, making amazing textures for cakes and pies. You can find it easily online and at some health food markets.

Makes 4 batches

What You'll Need
4 to 6 pieces Irish moss, soaked for 4 hours

2 tablespoons raw organic sesame oil

½ cup Almond Milk (page 58)

1 tablespoon lemon juice

Method
In a blender combine the soaked Irish moss, sesame oil, almond milk, and lemon juice, and blend until smooth (this will take a bit of time). Transfer the mixture to a bowl and set aside for 15 minutes to form a paste. If not using right away, you can store the paste in ice cube trays and cover with plastic wrap tightly, will keep in the freezer for up to 3 months.

Spirulina Sesame Bars

| high protein, filled with vitamin E, fiber rich |

Did you know spirulina is one of the best protein sources available? Is easily absorbs into the body and it doesn't cause your body to produce acid. Sesame seeds are one of the best ways to get calcium. Did you know that one cup of sesame seeds has more than three times the amount of calcium that milk does? And like spirulina, it does not cause any acid in the system that leads to calcium being leached from the bones. I love these bars as a pre- or post-gym snack!

Serves 8

What You'll Need

2 large bananas
1 tablespoon spirulina
1 tablespoon vanilla extract

1½ cups raw organic coconut shreds
1 cup raw organic sesame seeds
Pinch of salt

Method

In a food processor, combine the bananas, spirulina, vanilla, coconut, sesame seeds, and salt and blend for thirty seconds on high. Blend well until it's much like cookie dough. Spread the mixture on Teflex or dehydrator sheets to about ¼-inch thick. Dehydrate for 12 to 15 hours or until crisp.

Spice Milkshake

| healthy fat, blood sugar balancing, potassium |

This is a Thanksgiving-inspired recipe. I was on a liquid cleanse around the holiday and really wanted something that reminded me of pumpkin pie, so this delicious milkshake is what I came up with to satisfy my craving.

Serves 4

What You'll Need

4 cups unsweetened Cashew Milk
   (page 58)
3 frozen bananas
2 teaspoons pumpkin pie spice

½ teaspoon ground cinnamon
2 teaspoon vanilla extract
½ teaspoon sea salt

Method

In your blender combine cashew milk, bananas, pumpkin spice, cinnamon, vanilla, and salt. Blend until creamy, pour into glasses, and top with a bit of pumpkin spice. Enjoy!

BE MY DATE BARS

zinc, medium chain fatty acids, blood sugar balancing

I made up this recipe when I was about a month pregnant. I had given up chocolate and needed a treat to indulge in. My body was craving pumpkin seeds because they are really high in zinc. I love the cinnamon in this recipe; besides being a great flavor enhancer, it acts as a blood sugar balancer keeping your insulin levels from spiking. The dates that are in this recipe are a whole food containing fiber, which makes them easier for your body to digest and use as fuel, opposed to processed sugars.

Makes 12 slices

What You'll Need
5 to 8 organic dates, pitted and coarsely chopped
½ cup organic shredded coconut
¼ cup organic almonds
½ cup raw pumpkin seed butter
2 teaspoons ground cinnamon
½ teaspoon salt

Method
In a food processor, combine the dates, coconut, almonds, pumpkin seed butter, cinnamon, and salt. Process until a dough forms. Transfer the mixture onto a cutting board and shape into a loaf. Place in the freezer for ten minutes to chill. Take out and cut into bars to serve.

BRAZIL NUT FUDGE

selenium, magnesium, natural energy

This was another recipe I came up with during my pregnancy. I was seeing so many scrumptious pictures of food, and fudge was one of the things I had been craving. I felt good about eating this raw version for both me and my growing baby!

Makes 20 pieces

¾ cup raw organic Brazil nuts
½ cup raw organic almonds
⅓ cup pumpkin seed butter
2 medium dates, pitted
⅓ cup raw organic cacao powder
½ teaspoon maca
½ teaspoon mesquite powder
1 teaspoon vanilla extract
4 tablespoons coconut sugar
½ small ripe banana
½ teaspoon sea salt
½ cup raw organic cacao powder for topping

Method

In a food processor, combine the Brazil nuts and almonds. Process until a flour-like texture forms. Add the pumpkin seed butter, dates, cacao powder, maca, mesquite, vanilla, and coconut sugar. Blend well until moist and sticky. Add the banana and salt and process again to combine. Be aware that over processing will bring out the oil in the nuts and make the fudge hard to spread. Just process as needed.

Transfer the mixture onto parchment paper and use a spatula to spread it about ½-inch thick. If you would like a thicker fudge that's fine. It will just yield fewer pieces. Once it's spread, score the fudge into even squares and place in the freezer. The fudge should be set within one hour. Top with cacao powder and serve.

RAW POWER BARS

fiber rich, high protein, antioxidants

Most protein bars you find at the store are filled with fake sugars, dairy, and words you can't pronounce. This is a healthy alternative that will fuel your body and give you natural energy. Sunwarrior protein is one of my all-time favorite vegan proteins. I use it in my smoothies as well. It a wonderful clean and pure protein option for us vegans.

Makes 8 bars

What You'll Need
½ cup sprouted oat flour
¼ cup Walnut Flour (see page 247)
1 scoop vanilla Sunwarrior protein powder
1 teaspoon ground cinnamon
¼ cup chopped raw organic walnuts
½ medium banana
½ cup coconut sugar
3 tablespoons organic grade B maple syrup
1½ teaspoons vanilla extract
2 teaspoons almond extract
Pinch of salt
¼ cup fresh ground flax seed

Method
In a food processor combine the oat flour, walnut flour, protein powder, and cinnamon. Process well, then transfer to a bowl. Stir in the chopped walnuts and set aside.

In a high-speed blender, combine the banana, sugar, maple syrup, vanilla, almond extract, and salt. Fold the wet mixture into the dry mixture. Stir in the ground flax seed until well mixed.

Spread the mixture ¼- to ½-inch thick onto dehydrator sheets and cut into 1-inch by 2-inch bars. Dehydrate for 24 to 48 hours at 115 degrees. The timing will depend on the humidity and the thickness of your bar.

CLASSIC ALMOND BUTTER TRUFFLES

antioxidants, omegas, maca energy

When I first went raw, this is one of the simple chocolates I was obsessed with. Sometimes I mix it up and use different nut butters in place of almond. I love to add essential oils; peppermint and rose are my two favorites. Fave toppings include chopped pistachios, goji berries, cacao powder, rose petals, cinnamon, coconut sugar, and orange zest. This is a really fun process! Enjoy it.

Makes 15–20 truffles

What You'll Need

1 cup raw organic almond butter

4 tablespoons raw cacao powder

3 to 5 drops Stevia (to taste)

½ teaspoon vanilla extract

1 teaspoon maca

1 teaspoon sea salt

½ cup melted raw organic coconut oil

Method

In a high-speed blender, combine the first 6 ingredients. Then, add in the melted coconut and blend. Move to a bowl and refrigerate for 2 hours or overnight. Use an ice cream scoop to dish out even balls. Roll with your hands and then toss in your favorite topping. Once you've made your chocolates, keep them cool if not serving immediately.

Blissed Out Truffles

antioxidants, omegas, magnesium

This recipe is inspired by a recipe we used at the Matthew Kenney Academy. I remember chocolate day at the academy being so fun. Students really got inspired with their toppings. I hope you do the same! The options are endless.

Makes 15–20 truffles

What You'll Need
1 cup raw organic cashew butter
1 tablespoon vanilla extract
¼ cup coconut sugar
¼ cup maple syrup
¾ cup raw cacao powder
½ teaspoon sea salt
1 tablespoon melted raw organic coconut oil
3 tablespoons melted organic cacao butter

Method
In a high-speed blender blend together nut butter, vanilla, sweeteners, cacao powder, and salt. Blend well. Slowly add in coconut oil and melted cacao butter and blend. Transfer the mixture into a bowl and refrigerate for two hours or overnight. Scoop out truffles with an ice cream scoop. Roll into balls or shape with cookie cutters. Roll in your choice of toppings.

CHOCOLATE CARAMEL BARS

energizing, satisfying, mineral rich

These are another recipe I created for Local Juicery that is a total hit! People rave over these. They are an excellent way to indulge and not feel an ounce of guilt! I love making this for birthdays and special events.

Makes 9 slices

What You'll Need
Crust
8 cups walnuts
½ cup maple syrup
1 tablespoon vanilla extract
1 teaspoon sea salt
8 dates, pitted

Middle Layer
6 cups dry cashews
1 cup coconut oil

1 tablespoon vanilla
½ cup maple syrup
1 cup water
1 teaspoon sea salt

Topping
½ cup coconut butter
½ cup cacao butter
1 cup cacao powder
1 tablespoon Celtic salt

Method

For the Base
Line a large 9-inch square springform pan with plastic wrap and set aside.

Process walnuts, maple syrup, vanilla, salt, and dates gently, and pulse instead of a full blend. This mix should be chunky. Press into the bottom of the lined pan and put into the freezer.

For the Middle Layer
Process cashew, coconut oil, vanilla, maple syrup, water, and salt in a food processor on high. This mixture should be very, very creamy! Pour into the crust and bang it on the counter a bit to remove bubbles and even it out. Then return to the freezer.

For the Topping
On the stove top in a sauce pan, melt cacao butter with the coconut butter, and then add the cacao powder. This should be very silky. Once the clumps are melted out, pour over the bars and place in the freezer for 20 minutes. Top with Celtic sea salt.

CARROT CAKE

packed with vitamin A, protein, fiber

This is a wonderful recipe for Easter, children's birthdays, and spring picnics. The frosting can be colored using fruits and vegetables. It turns into a lovely pastel frosting. I love using carrot juice to color mine! You can make it as a cake or as cupcakes (a favorite of children).

Makes 4–8 slices

What You'll Need

1 cup grated carrot
½ cup grated green apple
1 cup raw organic walnuts, chopped
5 dates, pitted and chopped
½ cup coconut flakes
2 tablespoons coconut oil
¼ cup currants or dried cherries
¼ teaspoon mesquite powder
1 teaspoon vanilla extract
2 teaspoons ground cinnamon
1 teaspoon grated fresh ginger
⅛ teaspoon grated fresh nutmeg
1 tablespoon lemon juice
½ tablespoon lemon or orange zest
¼ teaspoon sea salt

Frosting

1 cup young coconut meat
½ cup coconut butter
½ medium banana
½ teaspoon vanilla extract
Pinch sea salt

Method

For the Cake

Combine the grated carrot and apple in the food processor and pulse until well combined. Add the walnuts, dates, coconut flakes, coconut oil, currants, mesquite, vanilla extract, cinnamon, ginger, nutmeg, lemon juice, zest, and sea salt. Pulse until a cake batter consistency forms. If the batter is too thin, add a little apple juice or water. Transfer the mixture to desired cake, springform, or cupcake pan.

Frosting

In a blender, combine the coconut meat, coconut butter, banana, vanilla, and salt and blend on high until the mixture is smooth and well combined. Pour or pipe the frosting onto the cake, spread over the cake, then refrigerate the cake to allow the frosting to firm up and chill. If you're making cupcakes, use a pastry bag or sandwich bag with a cut tip to decorate.

ALMOND BUTTER COOKIES

fiber, healthy fats, lowers ldl cholesterol

These are reminiscent of pecan sandies, they have the same crumbly texture. I really love this for post-workout snacks. They are super high in natural protein and give you energy when you need it most. They are also wonderful replacements for sugary cookies, making them a great alternative for children.

Serves 8

What You'll Need
1 cup Almond Flour (page 247)
¾ cup Sprouted Oat Flour (page 247)
Sea salt to taste
½ cup chopped raw organic almonds
½ cup raw organic almond butter
1 teaspoon almond extract
1 teaspoon vanilla extract
¼ cup organic grade B maple syrup
2 tablespoons coconut nectar

Method
Mix almond flour, oat flour, sea salt, and ¼ of the chopped almonds. Set aside. In your food processor, combine raw organic almond butter, extracts, and sweeteners. Slowly add in the dry mix. If you find that the mixture is a bit too dry, add water to your mix as needed while processing. Remember that it should not be too moist because it will take a long time to dehydrate.

Use an ice cream scoop and place on dehydrator sheets. Press down with a spoon and add reserved chopped raw organic almonds. Dehydrate for 12 to 24 hours at 115 degrees.

RAW PECAN BROWNIES

minerals, glutamine, oleic acid

Talk about a treat! You won't even know these are raw. Perfect for birthday parties and get-togethers. These are a tasty treat everyone will enjoy.

Makes 12 Brownies

¾ cup raw pecans, crushed
1 cup Oat Flour (see page 247)
2 cups Cashew Flour (page 247)
2 tablespoons almond butter
½ cup cacao powder
2 tablespoons vanilla extract
⅓ cup maple syrup
2 tablespoons coconut sugar
½ teaspoon sea salt
¾ cup raw organic cacao nibs, divided

Method

In a bowl, combine the pecans, oat flour, cashew flour, almond butter, cacao powder, vanilla, maple syrup, coconut sugar, and salt. Mix well by hand. Stir in 2 tablespoons of the cacao nibs. Form into 3-inch squares or desired shape and press the remaining nibs into the tops of the brownie. Dehydrate for 12 hours at 118 degrees. Store in a glass container in the refrigerator, and they keep for up to two weeks when stored correctly.

CLASSIC BERRY CHEESECAKE

antioxidants, protein, healthy fats

This is such an easy cheesecake to make. From the picture, you might think that it's complicated, but when I came up with this recipe it literally took seven minutes to execute. If you don't have coconut meat, that's okay, you can make this recipe without it. Just add a little extra cashew.

Makes 8–12 slices

What You'll Need
Perfect Pie Crust (page 175)
1½ cups raw organic cashews, soaked
⅓ cup raw honey or maple syrup, plus 1 tablespoon for berries
2 tablespoons coconut sugar
½ cup young coconut meat
⅓ cup lemon juice
1 teaspoon vanilla
1½ cups blackberries, frozen or fresh, divided
1½ cups raspberries, frozen or fresh, divided
½ to 1 teaspoon sea salt
Peaches, berries, or your favorite fruit, for topping

Method
Line a 9-inch springform pan with parchment paper or plastic wrap. Place the crust in the pan and press it down into the bottom of the pan. Set the crust in the freezer.

In a high-speed blender, combine the cashews, sweetner of choice, coconut sugar, coconut meat, lemon juice, vanilla, ½ cup of the blackberries, ½ cup of the raspberries, and the salt. Blend well, then slowly add the coconut oil and blend to combine. Pour the mixture into a 9-inch springform pan. Toss the remaining 2 cups of berries in 1 tablespoon of maple syrup and place on top of the cake. Place the cake in the freezer for 3 hours. Top with additional fresh fruit if desired.

LEMON LAVENDER TART

vitamin A, protein, mineral rich

This is a creamy taste bud pleaser and it's beautiful to look at. I love taking this to potlucks and dinner parties. People always want the recipe and are surprised when they learn that it's raw and vegan. The lavender adds an interesting flair to the taste and the berries really make it a visual delight.

Serves 8–12

What You'll Need
Perfect Pie Crust (page 175)
¼ cup dried or fresh lavender
⅓ cup raw honey
2 cups raw organic cashews, soaked
¾ cup raw organic coconut oil
¾ cup lemon juice
1 tablespoon lemon zest
1 tablespoon vanilla extract
½ to 1 teaspoon sea salt

Method
Press the pie crust into a 9 x 13-inch pie pan and then place it in the freezer.

Blend the lavender, water, and honey in a high-speed blender. Strain with a nut milk bag or strainer to remove the stems and flowers and set aside. In a high-speed blender, combine the cashews, coconut oil, reserved lavender honey mixture, lemon juice, lemon zest, vanilla extract, and sea salt. Blend until very smooth. Pour the mixture into the crust and return to the freezer to set (for about 2 hours). Just before serving, slice the lemons and place on the tart for decor.

DECADENT DARK CHOCOLATE GANACHE

protein, healthy fats, blood sugar balancing

My most favorite spot that I have ever visited is Oaxaca City in Mexico. Our good friends have a lovely home in the heart of the vibrant city and invited us to spend a Christmas with them. I was so inspired by the city; the colors, the flavors, the people, the art, the energy. I came home and this is what manifested in my kitchen.

Note: You can also prepare this recipe without the crust. It sets up very nicely in tumblers or wine glasses.

Makes 8–12 slices

What You'll Need
Perfect Pie Crust (page 175)
2 cups raw organic cashews, dry
1 cup coconut oil
1 cup raw organic cacao powder, plus 1 tablespoon for dusting
½ teaspoon cinnamon
¼–½ cup Almond Milk (page 58)
2 tablespoons vanilla extract
½ cup organic grade B maple syrup or coconut crystals
1 teaspoon sea salt
Assorted berries for topping

Method
Press the pie crust into a 9-inch pie pan and then place it in the freezer.

In a high-speed blender, blend cashews, coconut oil, cacao powder, cinnamon, almond milk, vanilla, maple syrup or coconut crystals, and salt. You may add more almond milk or water as needed. When a creamy consistency forms, pour into the prepared crust and then return the pan to the freezer to set for at least one hour. Once the tart is set, get a small strainer and dust cacao on it for a lovely topping.

Avocado Cacao Pudding

> fat burning, energizer, libido boost

This recipe is what we use at Local Juicery, and it's the best thing ever. I'm not kidding, women call me and have yelled at me when we've been out of it. I'm not messing around with this treat, it's the best one to serve to any raw food skeptics!

Makes 4–5 8oz servings

What You'll Need

5 ripe Hass avocados, pitted
2 cups soaked cashews
1 cup coconut oil
1 cup water, as needed
2 cups raw cacao powder
¼ cup maple syrup
¼ cup coconut sugar
1 tablespoon vanilla
½ tablespoon sea salt

Method

In your high-speed blender, combine the avocados, cashews, coconut oil and water. Blend until very creamy. Transfer to a food processor and add cacao, sweeteners, vanilla, and salt. Blend until well combined.

Serve in your favorite tumbler or dessert dish; this always looks lovely with fresh fruit and cacao nibs.

APPLE PIE TART

blood sugar balancing, fiber, minerals

This is a great holiday dish, and because it is put in the dehydrator for a short time, it even tastes a bit warm. I actually prefer this to cooked apple pie. Cinnamon is balancing for the blood sugar and keeps your insulin from spiking; it's a great spice to add to sweet treats.

Note: this is a smaller tart, and you can double the recipe to make a larger pie.

Makes 5 slices

½ recipe Perfect Pie Crust (page 175)
2½ large Fuji apples
1 tablespoon apple cider vinegar
1 teaspoon lemon juice
1 teaspoon vanilla extract
2 teaspoons ground cinnamon
¼ cup organic grade B maple syrup
¼ teaspoon sea salt

Method

Prepare ½ recipe of the pie crust. Press the crust into a 6-inch springform pan. Set aside.

Thinly slice the apples on a mandoline (or with a sharp knife) and set aside. In a bowl, combine the vinegar, lemon juice, vanilla, cinnamon, maple syrup, and salt. Blend with a whisk. Add the sliced apples and let marinate for five minutes.

Arrange the apple slices one at a time in the prepared pan, then transfer the tart to the dehydrator and dehydrate at 118 degrees for 35 minutes to soften.

Chaga Chai Latte

anti aging, antioxidants, immune support

Chaga is one of my favorite medicinal supplements. It has very high levels of antioxidants and is used by many to help suppress the growth of cancer. It has been called "the fountain of youth" and "the herb of the gods." It's very potent and nutritious. You can find it online and at many health food stores, and my own personal favorite is from Dragon Herbs.

Serves 4

What You'll Need
8 ounces favorite chai tea blend
4 ounces Raw Creamer (page 63)
4 Chaga mushroom capsules from Dragon Herbs
½ teaspoon ground cinnamon
2 tablespoons coconut sugar
Pinch of sea salt

Method
Brew a pot of chai tea, mix in the remaining ingredients and blend up quickly in a high-speed blender. Pour into a mug or mason jar. To get the froth on top, blend a bit of almond creamer on high. Pour on top and sprinkle with cinnamon.

PUMPKIN PIE CHEESECAKE

I created this pumpkin pie cheesecake so that I could enjoy the Thanksgiving holiday along with my family. It turned out to be a major hit and will be served as a tradition at our house for years to come. It's definitely rich, creamy, and delicious, I prefer it to traditional cheesecake! You can serve this cheesecake traditionally, made in a springform pan, or you can give it a different spin and serve it in 6 ounce mason jars.

Makes 8 slices or five 6-ounce mason jars

What You'll Need

Crust

1 ½ cups dry raw cashews

½ tablespoon molasses

1 tablespoon coconut oil

½ teaspoon vanilla

1 tablespoon fresh ginger, minced

1 tablespoon maple syrup or coconut sugar

½ teaspoon sea salt

Filling

2 ½ cups cashews, soaked

1 cup young coconut meat

2 tablespoons extra-virgin coconut oil

2 tablespoons coconut butter

½ cup carrot juice

2 teaspoons vanilla extract

1 ½ tablespoons pumpkin pie spice

1 tablespoon fresh ginger, grated

¾ to 1 cup coconut sugar

½ teaspoon molasses (not raw and optional)

¼ cup Walnut Milk or Pecan Milk (page 69, page 61)

2 ½ tablespoons lemon juice

½ to 1 teaspoon sea salt

Method

For the crust, blend all ingredients in a food processor until well combined. Press into the bottom of a 9-inch spring form pan or mason jars. Refrigerate until ready for use.

For the filling, blend soaked cashews, coconut meat, coconut oil, coconut butter, and carrot juice in your high-powered blender. Blend until smooth. Add remaining ingredients and combine.

Take out crust and pour filling into the pan. Let set in the freezer for 1 hour then transfer to the refrigerator.

Golden Milk

inflammation, immune boost, protein

This is a classic drink that has been given new energy in the past few years! It's a really amazing health tonic that I serve to my family just about every night. We also serve it at my juice bar, Local Juicery, and it's one of our most in-demand drinks. It's been compared to salted caramel ice cream! Enjoy warmed or cold. Make sure to add the black pepper for this is a carrier for turmeric—it activates the root and makes it work wonders for your body's health.

Serves 2

What You'll Need
16 oz. warm water
1 tablespoon turmeric powder or two small thumbs fresh turmeric
1 tablespoon coconut butter
1 tablespoon almond butter
1 tablespoon raw honey, or 7 drops Stevia
$\frac{1}{4}$ teaspoon black pepper
$\frac{1}{4}$ teaspoon cinnamon
$\frac{1}{8}$ teaspoon cardamom
$\frac{1}{4}$ teaspoon salt

Method
Blend warm water, turmeric, coconut butter, almond butter, sweetener, pepper, cinnamon, cardamom, and salt on high in your blender. Make sure it's frothy and well blended. Serve in your favorite cup with a dash of cardamom on top!

JUICES

Juice is my favorite way to get nutrients to my body. I usually start my day with thirty-two ounces of freshly juiced organic fruits and vegetables. I love pressed juice so much, I opened a cold-pressed juice bar! There is no quicker way to get your body cleaned out and filled with vitamins, antioxidants, and minerals. Even if I've fallen out of the groove with my routine and eating I always, *always* have my juice. There are two types of juicers available, centrifugal and masticating. Centrifugal is a lower-end juicer that heats up the juice and kills some of the enzymes in the grinding process. Masticating is a higher-end juicer that "chews" instead of grinds, preserving the vital nutrients and enzymes. There are also juice presses on the market that are proven to further protect the enzymes and important nutrition. You will benefit from the juice no matter what juicer you have or choose to buy, but if you can, try to steer toward a masticating juicer or a press.

I hope you enjoy these recipes I've created. They are my favorite daily juice recipes for health and gentle cleansing.

RECOVERY GREENS

alkalizing, hangover cure, immune boosting

This juice is great for a day of cleansing or getting back on the wagon with your healthy ways. I always drink this the day after I indulge in wine or non-raw foods.

Serves 4

What You'll Need

3 cups kale, shredded, tightly packed
4 chard leaves, stemmed
6 celery stalks
3 cups spinach, tightly packed
1 medium cucumber, peeled
1 small red bell pepper, stemmed and seeded
1 large lemon, peeled

Method

Juice kale, chard, celery, spinach, cucumber, bell pepper, and lemon. Pour into glass and serve.

THE EVERYTHING JUICE

skin saver, promotes weight loss, digestion aid

The name says everything; this is a full-on vitamin cocktail. I always say "eat your rainbow," but in this case, drink it. I love this juice when I'm doing a juice fast. I know that it gives me all the nutrients I need, a full spectrum of goodies!

Serves 4

What You'll Need
6 large carrots, washed and trimmed
4 medium oranges, peeled
½ small head purple cabbage (about 12 ounces)
1 small red beet, peeled
4 small green apples, cored
1 medium cucumber, peeled
4 leaves rainbow chard
1 medium piece ginger
1 large lime, peeled

Method
Juice all ingredients together. Pour into glasses and serve.

WATERMELON LIMEADE

energizing, cleansing, hydrating

Ask any of my friends, it is rare to find my house without a huge stockpile of watermelons. I love them. Only recently did I start turning this wonderful fruit into a juice.

Serves 4

What You'll Need
4 cups watermelon, chopped
3 tablespoons lime juice
Mint springs, for garnish

Method
In a high-speed blender, combine the watermelon chunks and lime juice. Blend until smooth. Pour into glasses and garnish with mint sprigs.

*Watermelon can also be run through a juicer if this is easier for you.

GREEN SPICE DETOX

liver, cellulite remover, kidney cleanser

The cranberries and jalapeño work together to help cleanse the blood and lymph system. I suggest drinking this juice in the morning, followed by ten minutes of skin brushing. This will really get the lymphatic system stimulated and help get rid of toxic buildup that creates cellulite.

Serves 4

What You'll Need
3 large green apples
8 celery stalks
2 large pears, cored
2 cups fresh or frozen cranberries
4 cups spinach, tightly packed
*¼ jalapeño, stemmed

Method
Juice apples, celery, pears, cranberries, spinach, and jalapeño. Pour into glasses and serve.

*Remove seeds if you prefer a mild juice.

I am Alive Green Juice

fights bad cholesterol, enzyme rich, hydrates

This juice is full of healthy enzymes that help your body properly break down and digest your food. The grapefruit helps with blood sugar and the cucumber is incredibly hydrating as well as alkalizing for the system. I suggest drinking this juice first thing in the morning. If pineapple is out of season or not available for you, try using papaya instead.

Serves 4

What You'll Need
2 large grapefruits, peeled
3 cups spinach, tightly packed
4 celery stalks

2 medium cucumbers, peeled
2 cups pineapple, chopped

Method
Juice grapefruits, spinach, celery, cucumber, and pineapple, pour into glasses, and serve.

Cantaloupe Cleanser

the hangover cure

This is a very moisturizing concoction that will rehydrate your cells and get you back in the groove of things. Very refreshing and cooling for the body.

Serves 4

What You'll Need
8 cups cubed cantaloupe
10 mint sprigs

½ cup water (if needed)
1 packet powdered Stevia (optional)

Method
Juice the cantaloupe and mint, adding water if needed. Mix in Stevia if it is not sweet enough for you. Remember, a little Stevia goes a long way! Chill for fifteen minutes in the refrigerator then serve.

Deep Root Cleansing Tonic

anti-inflammatory, heavy metal detoxifier, digestion aid

This is a highly cleansing recipe; it can really be beneficial for those with gut issues. This recipe is best enjoyed on an empty stomach. You can typically find coconut probiotics at health food stores. If not, online is great place to find it in powdered form.

Serves 4

What You'll Need
1 small thumb turmeric
1 small thumb ginger
5 large carrots
1 beet
½ cup liquid coconut probiotic (optional)
¼ teaspoon black pepper

Method
Juice turmeric, ginger, carrots, beet, and black pepper. Pour into a blender and blend probiotic in or stir by hand. Pour into glasses and serve.

THE LIGHT AND LOVE JUICE

alkalizing, immune boosting, liver flushing, glow giving

This drink for me is what light and love tastes like! Light, grounding, and so nourishing. Kids often love this one too!

Serves 4

What You'll Need
3 cups fresh spinach, tightly packed
2 cups shredded kale, tightly packed
2 fennel stalks, coarsely chopped
2 large cucumbers, peeled
2 Bartlett pears, cored and quartered
2 large limes, peeled
1 cup peppermint leaves

Method
Juice spinach, kale, fennel, cucumber, pears, limes, and peppermint. Pour into glasses and serve.

VENICE JUICE

energizing, hydration, awakening

Venice Beach is full of life, full of artists, full of creative minds. I created this juice when I first moved to Venice, inspired by the ocean, the people, and the energy. It's a super hydrating juice that gives you the energy for hours to do whatever it is your creative self feels like exploring.

Serves 4

What You'll Need

1 cup pineapple, peeled, cored, and chopped

4 large oranges, peeled

3 cups fresh spinach, tightly packed

2 cups young coconut water

Method

Juice the pineapple, oranges, and spinach. Add to coconut water in a pitcher and stir. Serve cold.

BEET OF MY HEART

blood building, liver cleansing, natural energy

Beet juice is a total blood builder; it also cleanses the liver and acts as a mild laxative. If you're needing a full body tone-up from the inside out, this is the juice for you!

Serves 4

What You'll Need

2 medium red beets, peeled and quartered

3 large green apples, cored and quartered

4 cups shredded kale, tightly packed

2 cups fresh spinach, tightly packed

1 medium lemon, peeled

Method

Juice the beets, apples, kale, spinach, and lemon. Serve immediately.

BODY BALANCER

hormone balancing, warming, blood sugar balancing

This super-tasty juice is inspired by my favorite juice bar in the world! Moon Juice in Venice Beach, California. When I lived in Venice I went to Moon Juice every day. They have really unique combinations of juices and they are all cold pressed. If you ever get to Venice Beach, make sure to check it out!

Serve 2–3

What You'll Need

3 medium yams, peeled and quartered
4 medium red apples, cored and quartered
1 large lemon or lime, peeled
2 cups young coconut meat, packed tightly
1 teaspoon ground cinnamon

Method

Juice the yams, apples, and lemon. Pour the juice into a high-speed blender and then blend with the coconut meat and cinnamon. If you don't have access to coconut meat, you can make this juice without or you can add a bit of Coconut Milk (page 64). Pour into glasses and serve.

PART III.
THE
CLEANSE

CLEANSING

Our bodies tend to store toxins. Whether it's from chemicals in products we use, pesticides in our foods, medications, or bad living habits, we have buildup in our bodies that inhibit optimum health, keep unwanted weight on our bodies, and create a breeding ground for disease. I believe in doing gentle and supportive cleanses at least once a year. Think of it this way: You take your car to get its oil changed every three thousand miles, don't you? You update the software on your computer to make sure it's running at the right speed, right? Think of cleansing as that—a tune up for your body! I strongly recommend staying away from hardcore cleanses that can wreck your digestion and colon function. Always best to see a natural health care professional before you start any kind of cleanse.

WHY SHOULD I CLEANSE?

Like I said, think of cleansing as a tune up. Your body needs a break from constantly working. The majority of us have colons that are full of stagnant toxins. The goal is to have healthy bowel movements at least two times a day, and three is even better. If you have less than this, you have some cleaning out to do! This cleanse will help. The point of cleansing is to reset, renew, and restore the body to a healthy and thriving state.

WHAT DO I NEED?

A juicer or a juice bar that is nearby your home or work place, and a strong blender such as a Vitamix or Blendtec. You'll need to stock up on greens and fruits (kale, spinach, dandelion greens, beets, beet top greens, parsley, peeled cucumber, apples, lemons, papaya, watermelon, homemade raw almond milk). See the grocery list (page 24) for more ideas. You'll need an enema bag or a few appointments at a colon hydro-therapist. Bring your willpower and positivity!

HOW LONG SHOULD I CLEANSE FOR?

This is a gentle five-day juice and smoothie cleanse. Its purpose is to clean out your body and prepare you for a plant-based lifestyle. It is safe to continue this cleanse for longer, if you wish. As with any new way of eating or cleansing, I suggest consulting with your doctor before embarking on this cleanse. I would suggest seeing a naturopath instead of a traditional allopathic doctor. Naturopaths tend to be more versed in the practice of using food as medicine, and will support your holistic approach to healing.

WHAT CAN I EXPECT?

Most people experience low energy for the first three days of cleansing. Taking enemas or colonics during the cleanse will help with this. I know this is unappealing to many people and can be intimidating, but while you are cleansing it is important and very beneficial. Since you are not eating fiber, you will need to move the toxins out, and enemas and colonics are the best way to do this. (See page 225 for more on colon cleansing) Remember, it is crucial to be drinking plenty of water; this helps with the elimination of toxins.

> "The way out is through."
>
> —Michael Brown, author of the *Presence Process*

After the third day, you will begin to feel energized and your cravings will start to subside. You can expect to lose some weight on this cleanse. Some of this weight will be water weight and some of it will be fat. It's important to know that if you do this cleanse and afterwards continue to eat exactly how you were eating before, you will gain all that weight back.

Be aware that often when cleansing, there is an emotional detox that occurs as well—this is a good thing. Be gentle and compassionate with yourself; consider meditation and deep breathing to support you with this. See book recommendations (on page 248) for more support with the emotional aspect of cleansing. Most people spend their life talking about getting in shape and being healthy. Few actually make it happen! Be the exception.

HOW TO DO AN ENEMA

I really support all my clients and anyone who is cleansing or wanting to reach the next level of health to try out an enema. Getting old, putrefying waste out of your body can't help but promote healing and weight loss. Here are instructions for self-facilitated enemas.

WHAT YOU'LL NEED

1. Enema bucket or bag
2. Coconut or olive oil for lubricating

OPTIONAL INGREDIENTS

1. 1½ quarts pure water (boiled or distilled) that is warm to the touch, but not boiling hot!
2. ¼ cup fresh juiced greens, something with chlorophyll or lemon juice. This is optional, you can just do water if that is easiest.
3. A pure probiotic formula, therapeutic strength with predominantly Bifodobacteria species – 4-5 billion viable cells (to replace the health promoting bacteria). After enema is finished, add this to a small amount of water and hold inside intestines.

Directions: Mix the above ingredients together, recheck the temperature of the solution, and instill the solution into the rectum.

HOW TO TAKE AN ENEMA

1. Place solution in your enema bucket or bag (valve closed).
2. Open valve to fill tube and remove any air bubbles in the tube, close valve, and lubricate the tip of the tube as well as the opening to your rectum.
3. Place the enema bag on somewhere that it is held and will not move. On several bath towels, lay down on your left side in the knee-chest/fetal position (a bath during enema is a great way to relax). Gently and steadily insert the enema tube into the rectum—approximately 6 to 12 centimeters for adults and 3 to 4 centimeters for children, with the tip pointing towards your navel.
   Warning: Do not force the tip. If you experience resistance, change the angle and try again.
4. Open the valve and let the solution flow into your rectum as much as tolerated. It helps to massage the abdomen to relax the colon and allow filling, especially if it becomes uncomfortable. A small amount of liquid may remain in the bucket. It is not necessary to completely empty the contents of the bag, you can do two or three rounds. I suggest refilling the bag when it is empty and doing two rounds. Close the valve and remove the tube when you are done.
5. Rest on your left side or on your back with knees bent for 1 to 5 minutes (as long as possible) and gently massage your abdomen before getting up to evacuate on the toilet.
6. Wash the enema bucket and the tube with soap and hot water following each use. Additionally, you can rinse it with hydrogen peroxide.

THE FOUNDATION CLEANSE

This five-day mild detox is a guide that I use for myself and for my clients. It will help support you on your journey to health. It is a simple and gentle cleanse that is easy to follow and most importantly, not shocking for your body. I don't believe in harsh cleanses. The body is a delicate system that is doing its best to stay healthy. By removing these toxic foods, habits, and ideas, we help our bodies reset and support them to rebuild their foundations.

BEFORE YOU BEGIN

You will need plenty of fruits and veggies for this cleanse. You can use the recipes I have provided here or in the Juices section (pages 207) and the Smoothies section (page 73), they are effective in cleansing and weight loss. Another option is to make up your own recipes using fruits and vegetables of your choice. If you will be going to a juice bar, be sure they are using only organic produce, even better if they are cold pressed! If you choose to use your own recipes, make sure to use plenty of organic leafy greens and bitter herbs such as dandelion. You will also need a skin brush, enema kit, and probiotics. You can find skin brushes and enema bags online or often at your local health food store. These tools help remove toxins and support you to fully cleanse.

The Plan

DAY ONE

Morning: Probiotic followed by warm water with lemon or lime.
Wheatgrass shot if available (powdered wheatgrass is a fine substitute)
Green Lemonade Juice: ½ head romaine lettuce, large handful spinach, 1 lemon or lime, 3 celery stalks, 1 cucumber, 1 green apple

Mid-Morning: Goji Milk or Almond Milk (pages 58)

Afternoon: Glow Smoothie: 1 cup water, ½ avocado, handful kale, 1 tablespoon lemon juice, small thumb ginger, frozen blueberries, ½ frozen banana, Stevia to taste, pinch of sea salt.

Mid-Afternoon: Beet baby juice: 1 beet, 1 carrot, 2 limes, and coconut water.

Evening: Juicy Juice: 1 cup water, 3 kale stalks, 1 banana, 1 orange, 3 tablespoons hemp seeds, pinch of sea salt, Stevia to taste.

Dessert: Almond milk with cacao powder blended. Add a bit of coconut sugar for sweetener.

Notes: I suggest starting at 7:00 a.m. and having your last drink by 7:00 p.m. If you want more juice, feel free! Drink as much tea and water as you want—no coffee though! Do yoga, squats, and push-ups, rest when tired, and read a good book. Don't forget to post pictures—use the hashtag #rawandradiant!

DAY TWO

Morning: Probiotic followed by warm water with lemon or lime. Wheatgrass shot if available.

Green Lemonade Juice: ½ head romaine lettuce, large handful spinach, 1 lemon or lime, 3 celery stalks, 1 cucumber, 1 green apple.

Mid-Morning: Papaya or melon smoothie: cut up papaya or melon and blend with water (at least one cup).

Afternoon: Cacao Super Smoothie: 1 cup almond milk, ½ avocado, handful spinach, 3 tablespoons cacao powder, ½ frozen banana, ½ teaspoon maca. Stevia to taste, pinch of sea salt.

Mid-Afternoon: Kale Punch: large bunch kale, 2 green apples, 3 celery stalks, 2 limes, and coconut water.

Evening: 1 cup water, 1 head of romaine lettuce, 1 banana, 1 whole orange, 3 tablespoons hemp seeds, pinch of sea salt.

Dessert: Almond milk with cacao powder blended. Add a bit of coconut sugar for sweetener.

Or fresh apple juice blended with cinnamon, a banana, and a pinch of salt.

DAY THREE

Morning: Probiotic followed by warm water with lemon or lime. Wheatgrass shot if available

Green Lemonade Juice: ½ head romaine lettuce, large handful spinach, 1 lemon or lime, 3 celery stalks, 1 cucumber, 1 green apple.

Mid-Morning: Juice: Apple, spinach, and cucumber juice with coconut water

Afternoon: Tropical Breeze: 1 cup coconut water, 1 banana, 3 kale stalks, 1 cup frozen mango, goji berries, pinch of sea salt.

Mid-Afternoon: Green Dream Juice: Celery, spinach, chard or kale, orange, green apple.

Evening: Strawberry Warrior: 1 cup water, 1 cup frozen strawberries, 1 scoop warrior protein or 3 tablespoons hemp seeds, ½ frozen banana, favorite green supplement, pinch of salt.

Dessert: Almond milk with cacao powder blended. Add a bit of coconut sugar for sweetener.

Or fresh apple juice blended with cinnamon, a banana, and a pinch of salt.

DAY FOUR

Morning: Probiotic followed by warm water with lemon or lime. Wheatgrass shot if available

Green Lemonade Juice: ½ head romaine lettuce, large handful spinach, 1 lemon or lime, 3 celery stalks, 1 cucumber, 1 green apple or any variation of this.

Mid-Morning: Sweet Cinnamon: 1 cup almond milk with cinnamon, clove, maca, Stevia, and vanilla.

Afternoon: Blueberry Crush: 1 cup coconut water, 1 banana, 1 cup frozen blueberries, 2 tablespoons hemp seeds, 1 tablespoon honey, 1 tablespoon bee pollen, pinch of sea salt. *Bee pollen and honey can be taken out if vegan.

Mid-Afternoon: Classic Juice: Cucumber, spinach, romaine lettuce, lemon, green apple.

Evening: Superfood Smoothie: 1 cup favorite nut milk (walnut is mine!), 1 cup frozen or fresh pineapple, 5 large pieces lettuce, goji berries, coconut flakes, maca, camu camu, Stevia if needed, pinch of salt.

Dessert: Almond milk with cacao powder blended. Add a bit of coconut sugar for sweetener.

Or Coconut milk (coconut shreds, coconut sugar, salt, water, blended and strained) with cinnamon or vanilla.

DAY FIVE

IMPORTANT: When you break a fast or cleanse, it's very important to be gentle with what you eat. The first day, do only smoothies, fruit, and then a large salad. Never break a fast with toxic food such as pizza. Be gentle with your body!

Morning: Probiotic followed by warm water with lemon or lime.

Wheatgrass shot if available

Green Lemonade Juice: ½ head romaine lettuce, large handful spinach, 1 lemon or lime, 3 celery stalks, 1 cucumber, 1 green apple or any variation of this.

Mid-Morning: 1 cup coconut water, 2 tablespoons lime juice, 1½ cups frozen strawberries, Stevia to taste.

Afternoon: Citrus Rush: 1 cup grapefruit juice (fresh), 1 tablespoon lemon juice, 1 frozen banana, ½ head romaine lettuce, 2 dates, pinch of maca, and salt.

Mid-Afternoon: Bunny-C: 4 carrots, 2 oranges, large bunch spinach, 1 cucumber.

Evening: Calcium Yum: 1 cup almond milk, 1 tablespoon tahini, 2 table spoons cacao, ½ teaspoon maca, spinach, maple syrup or Stevia to taste, pinch of salt.

Dessert: Coconut milk (coconut shreds, coconut sugar, salt, water, blended and strained) with cinnamon or vanilla.

Feel free to mix match all of these! The goal is to have an abundance of fresh, leafy, vibrant greens. Make sure you are drinking a good amount of water. You can also drink lemon water or cranberry water whenever you would like.

MAKE IT COUNT

As a companion to the cleanse, I suggest reading a book that supports what you're doing on an emotional and physical level. When it's time to break your fast, be very careful. You don't want to shock or stress your body. Take two days to ease back into eating with raw fruits and veggies. Then gradually add back in whole grains and foods that are a part of your healthy eating plan. Remember, enemas and colon cleansing are vital to cleansing and really getting the toxins out of your body. If you don't do an enema (see page 223 for direction and recipes), then you run the risk of having these toxins come out in other ways such as breakouts.

People in your life may not understand what you're doing, or may be jealous that you're taking time for yourself. Be a positive enforcer, help educate these people. You are leading by example. Again, don't forget the power of one, it is indeed very powerful.

PART IV.
BECOMING
STRONG + RADIANT

Natural Skin and Body Care

My experience with beauty is that the most radiant women have a glow that comes from within. It's not skin-deep in any way. The ladies I know who glow, feed themselves lovingly both with their self-talk and their food. Cultivating self-love first and foremost, and then feeding your body with love is definitely my preferred route to radiant beauty.

"Though we travel the world over to find the beautiful, we must carry it with us or we find it not."

—Ralph Waldo Emerson

It is really important to make sure that the products you use on your skin are clean and chemical-free. Remember your skin is the largest organ in your body. This means whatever you put on it is then taken into the body and processed though the liver and kidneys. I have a comprehensive list on my website, www.strongandradiant.com, of the chemicals to steer clear of. Below I'll share some of my favorite foods and products for dewy, glowy, youthful skin.

Foods + Beauty Products

Barley grass (blood cleanser)
Cucumber (hydrating)
Figs (calcium)
Hemp hearts (omegas)
Melons (hydrating)
Neem (skin-saving)
Raw organic pumpkin seeds (zinc)
Sprouts (sulfur)
Wheatgrass (oxygenating)
Young coconut water (hydrating)

Apple cider vinegar (alkalizes the body and skin's ph levels)
Avocado oil (cures dry skin)
Baking soda (exfoliates and alkalizes the skin)
Coconut oil (hydrates skin and hair)
Macadamia nut oil (moisturizes and renews skin)
Olive oil (vitamin E)
Papaya (skin brightener)
Coconut (natural antiseptic)

My Favorite Natural Beauty Products

Jiva apoha oils
Nucifera balm
Rms makeup
Living libations
Osmia organics
Herbivore

Mychelle
Isun
Mineral fusion
Bentonite clay (clears pores)
Tata harper
Ajai

GET ACTIVATED WITH PASSIONS

Do you know what your passions are? I mean that deep, burning passion that sets your heart on fire? If you're not quite sure what it is, a good way to get in touch with yourself is to think back to what it was that made you feel amazing as a child. What was it that made/makes you come alive?

Often, we don't give time and space to the things that our soul is craving and this can slowly chip away at our health, both mental, emotional, and physical. Some of us are blessed to have a clear vision of what our passion is and some are even blessed to work in those passions. Just because you don't work in your passion for your monetary means, doesn't mean you shouldn't spend time on it. Maybe your passion is music but you never touch a piano or sing. Find just five minutes a day to feed yourself in this way and I know you'll start to feel a change in your life.

By using your talents, you bless the world! If you have a killer voice, sing out! If you can write poetry that brings people to tears, do it. If making pottery brings you joy, make those bowls! It's not about doing it for money necessarily, though when you give passions time and attention, they often can lead to that.

CONNECTED AFFIRMATIONS

The other day I was talking to my four-year-old son (pictured) and he said to me, "Mama, I'm awesome!" It wasn't a conceited statement; his face was full of joy and he truly—to his core—knew that he was indeed awesome. How lovely and how beautiful for us adults to get back to that innocent place of loving ourselves and seeing our divinity, as my son and so many children do. Working with affirmations can be a wonderful supplement to our other self-care and inner work. These affirmations might seem unrelated to your passion, but if you can find a time to repeat them or post them on your wall where you will see them often, you will find that your passions and creative self will begin to show up more in your life. I'm a fan of repeating positive things to myself . . . I make sure that when I'm saying these, they aren't just empty words, that I'm really feeling the things I'm saying. Affirmations alone won't change much if you are not able to really dig deep and hold space for the feelings and life you want to manifest.

I let go of the fear of judgment and breathe in love.
I choose to forgive and let love fill my body.
I am not my body; I am eternal grace, and loving light.
I choose to live my life passionately.
I see everyone as they are, perfect beings made by the spirit.
I am not my story; I choose to shift my perspective.
I drop my judgments of others, and myself, and choose to see love instead.
I open my heart to the miracle that I am.
Every moment has a lesson; I open my heart to the teachings of the now.
I am love.

These affirmations have power when said with belief. Let them really sink in.

RITUALS

Rituals can be as simple as lighting a candle in the evening, or as extravagant as herbal soak baths and hour-long meditations. It really just depends on what your personal time constraints and needs are. For me, as a busy mama and business owner, it's really about finding rituals that hold me, give me deep self-care, and remind me to turn inward without taking up hours of my day. If you're just beginning to bring sacred rituals into your life, I suggest turning to the mornings. The early morning is powerful and helps set the tone for the rest of your day. Health goes far beyond physical. The trinity of mind, body, and spirit all play an equal part in vibrant health. Here are some examples of rituals you can work into your day and bring balance to your life.

- Breathing. I love doing fifteen minutes of deep, connected breathing.
- Lighting natural incense, palo santo, or sage to clear the house and cleanse the air, just the act of this can bring awareness to your core.
- Reading a passage from a book or poem that feeds you, spiritually, mentally, and emotionally.
- Brewing your favorite herbal tea and enjoying the sunrise or set.
- A warm bath.
- Lighting a candle and doing a meditation.
- Yoga.
- Saunas or steams.
- Walk outside in nature.
- Listen to calm and sweet music.

All of these are acts of self-love. It's easy to be in a hurry, running in circles, trying to get from A to B. If you only have time for one ritual that's okay, integrate it into your morning and you will feel a difference. Make it a priority. It will help that path from A to B become clear and less stressed. We all need time to reflect, look inward, and feel gratitude for our existence. Start your day out with what you feel is most important for you. This will serve you and the people around you immensely. Share your rituals with me online at #rawandradiant.

MOVEMENT

Being active is vital not only for creating a healthy and strong body, but for emotional health as well. Go outside for just ten minutes and do some pushups and jumping jacks, and you will feel your mood improve significantly. It's amazing what a little movement can do. I'm a certified personal trainer and my husband is in the military, so physical fitness is a part of our daily lives. We both believe in functional fitness, meaning we do exercises that apply to our lives and help build our muscles for practical things that we will actually engage in. Many people feel that they cannot commit to a fitness routine because they need a gym membership and can't afford it, or don't have a gym nearby. However, there are so many workouts you can do that require only your body! Doing body weight exercises, stretching, and outdoor cardio are wonderful "free" ways to get into the best shape of your life.

Yoga

I practice yoga at least three times a week, whether at home or at a studio. I've found that this is the magic number to really see and feel the results for my body. I enjoy hot yoga (typically a Vinyasa Flow) as well as hatha yoga. Most cities and towns have yoga studios. Look for a studio that offers classes during a time that you would truthfully attend. If you have the luxury, I would suggest that you try a few different studios. Finding the right teacher for your needs can be a task. You can also buy a DVD, crank up the heat, and do your flow at home. You can even find yoga on YouTube these days!

Yoga benefits the mind, body, and spirit. It is great for building long, lean muscles, strengthening your core, relaxing, and cleansing the body. Yoga has a way of elevating your mood and it's not just in your head! A study from Boston University School of Medicine and McLean Hospital reports that during one hour of asana, participants raised their levels of GABA (acts as inhibitory neurotransmitter that supports calm and peacefulness in the body) by more than 25 percent compared with a group who read quietly. Yoga is also great for your sex life. Yoga helps reduce anxiety, increases blood flow, speeds up the release of hormones that promote arousal, and it connects you to your body. All of this helps your libido. It's worth a try!

Weight Training

A common misperception many women have is that lifting weights will make them bulky and masculine. This is not true. Lifting weights will build bone density, burn calories, and shed unwanted fat, while allowing your body to gain muscle. Muscle burns more calories than fat, and building up your muscles will raise your resting metabolic rate (the number of calories your body burns when just sitting on the couch). Weight training is a necessity in my life; it has changed the shape of my body completely. I suggest hiring a personal trainer to help teach you form and proper movements.

When beginning a weight training program, start with three days a week. Once you become confident and feel your body becoming stronger, you can train more frequently. I like to supplement my weight training with hikes, outdoor cardio, swimming, and walks. There are some great online resources for weight training. I love www.fitnessrxwomen. com and www.oxygen.com; they have great training programs, videos, and instructions for proper form. As you'll see on these websites, a very high protein diet is usually recommended. I personally don't believe this is needed to build healthy muscles—vegan protein from hemp, nuts, seeds, and whole food supplements are just as good for building strong muscles.

Body Weight

Using your own body weight for workouts is a safe and effective way to work out without a gym, and builds strength. As a Naval Officer, my husband holds himself as well as his men to very high physical standards. He often uses his own body weight for his workouts. The great thing about body weight exercise is that it is progressive. You can start slow at your own pace and, when you're ready, you build up to an incredibly hard workout. Some examples of body weight exercises are: pushups, sit ups, pull ups, pistols, and handstands. I love using these when I'm traveling; no need for a gym or any equipment!

CrossFit

CrossFit is one of my favorite workouts. It's very high intensity, explosive, and quick. Your standard CrossFit workout is thirty minutes. It's based on the idea that our ancestors (the cavemen) lifted big rocks, logs, and ran in short bursts, instead of spending two hours in the gym working on every body part, CrossFit gets it all done at once. I love pairing it with yoga. The blend of CrossFit and yoga is my all-time favorite workout combination. I get the burst of energy and body toning I need from the CrossFit and the stretch and mindfulness that is important to my well-being from yoga.

There are many CrossFit gyms all over the US, Canada, and Europe. It's important to find a gym that really focuses on form; without good form you can really damage your body and hurt yourself. Take it slow and follow good form always!

Running

Running is a wonderful way to elevate your mood, clear your mind, and get your lungs pumping oxygen to your brain and heart. Start slowly with your runs. I suggest doing a walk/run routine when you're first getting started. I love using a heart rate monitor watch to track my miles. I suggest to my clients to start slow with one mile depending on their current level of cardio vascular fitness. If you are just beginning, the run/walk method will be a perfect starting point. Walk the first three minutes and then run the next three. Change off every three minutes. Do this three days a week and up your mileage each week until you get to three-plus miles per run.

Sprints are an amazing way to cut fat and get your workout done really quickly. Sprinting is when you run all out as fast as you can for short bursts. The best way to do this is find a track or grassy field. I like to do twenty- to thirty- second sprints and then walk it out for one minute. I do this for fifteen minutes minimum and it's incredibly hard, but satisfying and so effective. Make sure to fuel up with a superfood smoothie afterwards!

ENTERTAINING

Dinner Parties, Birthdays, and More

My favorite thing about food is the company. Nothing brings me more joy than being surrounded by my best friends and family. There are so many wonderful occasions worth celebrating and they are great opportunities to share your love of raw food with the ones you care about. Here are a few tips that have helped me when planning meals for large groups and special occasions.

- Plan ahead. Get a count of people who will be attending the function.
- Ask those attending about allergies and food aversion.
- Start your prep two days before the actual event.
- Save salads, fresh fruits, and veggies for last.
- If you see you might be overwhelmed, call on a friend or family member for help.
- Plan your menu based on the season. You are more likely to find local and unique ingredients to make your dinner parties unforgettable.
- Consider setting it up buffet style with little cards explaining what you are serving with a list of key ingredients.

APPENDICES

SOAKING

Soaking and sprouting are an important part of the raw food diet. This can seem intimidating to a busy person. Sprouting? Soaking? Who has time to do all of that? I felt that way at the beginning of my raw food journey. I came to realize that once you get things on a rotation, it takes no more than ten minutes out of your day, and it is ten minutes that could potentially be adding years to your life. I would say it's worth it. I always soak them in the refrigerator to keep bacteria from growing.

Here is how to soak.

You will need to soak all your nuts and seeds before you use them. You will also want to soak any steel cut oats and organic buckwheat. Nuts (besides hazelnuts and Brazil nuts) have enzyme inhibitors in their skin, and by soaking them, the inhibitors are released and you are left with an easy-to-digest, protein-packed, and nutrient-dense superfood! Most nuts need to be soaked for at least five hours. I always suggest letting them soak overnight. I also soak them in the refrigerator to keep bacteria from growing.

Nuts often harbor molds and bacteria due to their fat content. To clean the grains, nuts, or seeds of these not-so-welcomed guest, I suggest using food grade hydrogen peroxide. For every eight ounces of water, use ¼ teaspoon of hydrogen peroxide. Let the nuts or seeds sit in the peroxide for one minute, then rinse well. The cleaning process is easier if done before the soaking is started.

I always suggest soaking raw organic almonds for at least twenty-four hours. They have an especially tough exterior and are harder on the digestive system. The longer they soak, the easier they are to digest. Make sure to soak them in the refrigerator!

What You'll Need
Glass jars for soaking
A strainer
Food grade hydrogen peroxide
Filtered water
Measuring cup

Method
Measure out the amount of nuts or seeds you need. For every 8 ounces of nuts or seeds, use 16 ounces of water. Use ¼ teaspoon of hydrogen peroxide to every 8 ounces of water. After cleaning, store in the refrigerator while soaking. Let them soak for five hours minimum.

Sprouting

By sprouting your nuts, seeds, and grains, you reduce phytic acid. Phytic acid is a nutrient blocker that is found in most nuts, seeds, and grains. It keeps your body from getting all the important minerals and vitamins that are in these foods. The phytic acid binds to the food and in binding, does not let the vital nutrients pass into your bloodstream. The solution to this is easy! Sprout all your nuts, seeds, and grains.

What You'll Need
A gallon glass jar
Cheesecloth or netting
Rubber-band

Method
Cover nuts, seeds, or grains with filtered water and soak overnight. The next day, drain the water out, rinse with filtered water and drain again. Cover the mouth of your jar with cheesecloth or netting and keep in place with a rubber band. Let the jar sit on your counter (in the darkest spot) for one to two days or until you start to see a little sprout. You can turn the jar on its side if you want more room for the sprouts, this also allows more air flow, helping to prevent mold. If mold is a concern for you, put a small house fan near the mouth of the jar while they sit over-night. The air flow will help. Be sure to rinse and drain the jar a few times each day, remembering to always use filtered water. Once you see the little tip of the sprout, your process is done.

Raw Flours

You can still make cookies, breads, and pastries, while staying true to a raw food diet. I eat these goodies only on occasion, but I find it so wonderful that I can still indulge in a chocolate chip cookie now and again. Flour in raw food is usually made out of sprouted oats, organic buckwheat, or nuts.

Making Flours

For flours made out of nuts, the process can vary. For cashew flour, put the unsoaked dry raw cashews in the blender and blend very quickly on high. If you blend for too long, it can become a butter. For almond flour, there are two ways to prepare it. One is to use the pulp from almond milk, dehydrate it, and blend it into flour. For finer flour, you can sift the meal.

The other method is to blend soaked and dehydrated (dried) raw organic almonds into a rough flour; this can be sifted or left textured. You can use this method with most nuts. The more oil the nut has, the harder it is to make a flour. Follow the cashew method for oilier nuts.

The process for making the flour out of oats and buckwheat is the same. Soak and sprout the groats, dehydrate them, and blend on high until flour forms. I often sift my flour to make a delicate texture that works great for pastries and cakes if I'm working on a more complex recipe.

FAVORITE READING & RESOURCES

Nutrition Food Books

Everyday Raw Detox by Meredith Baird and Matthew Kenney
Coconut Kitchen by Meredith Baird
Eating for Beauty by David "Avocado" Wolfe
Rawsome! by Brigitte Mars
Rainbow Green Live-Food Cuisine by Dr. Gabriel Cousens
Survival into the 21st Century by Viktoras H.Kulvinskas
Crazy Sexy Diet by Kris Carr
Nutrition Stripped by Mckhil Hill
Medical Medium by Anthony William

Emotional and Spiritual

The Presence Process by Michael Brown
The Power of Now by Eckhart Tolle
Loving What Is by Byron Katie
The Desire Map by Danielle Laporte
A Course in Miracles

Food Documentaries

The Garden
Forks Over Knives
Food Matters
King Corn
Food Inc.
The Future of Food

Favorite Websites and Blogs

www.strongandradiant.com
www.mindbodygreen.com
www.wellandgood.com
www.ourbodybook.com
www.superfoodsuperlife.com
www.thechalkbaordmag.com
www.dahlhousenutriton.com
www.vidyaliving.com
www.freeandnative.com
www.sakaralife.com
www.houseofcitrine.com

Favorite Health Products

Omica Vanilla Stevia
Organic India Psyllium Husk
Great Plains Bentonite Detox Clay
Sun Potion Tonic Herbs
2Rise Naturals CBD Oil
Quantum Nutrition Labs
Life Extension Supplements
Bulletproof Coffee and Supplements
Philosophie Mama Protein and Superfoods
Moon Juice Moon Pantry
Moon Deli Tonic Herbs
Essential Medicina Medicinal Blends
Mattole Valley Goat and Plant Protein

Education

www.matthewkenneycuisine.com
www.treeoflife.nu.
www.integrativenutrition.com
www.ecornell.com

ACKNOWLEDGMENTS

I want to acknowledge the entire healthy living community. There are so many wonderful, beautiful, and heartfelt people making a difference with their love for real food and healing. It is great to be in a line of work that is so connected and purposeful.

My sweet family, my mom, my dad, my son, and my husband, my mother- and father-in-law . . . You all have helped this book come to life and I so appreciate your constant love and support. You are what it's all about.

Lyrica Tyree thank you for being my best friend and inspiring me to follow through. Your eye for detail and patience is rare. You're a true artist.

Kendra, it has been an honor to be your friend. By watching you start 2rise Naturals, I have learned so much about health, heart, and happiness. I love you dearly.

Nicole, Michelle, and the entire Branch family, thank you for your love and support and mutual respect for healthy foods. I love you all so much.

Meredith Baird, you have been a big inspiration to me whether you know it or not. You are effortless in your beauty and a true artist when it comes to food. I'm grateful to know you.

Thank you to Matthew Kenney for inspiring and making raw food a beautiful cuisine, not just hippie fare (though, I do love hippie fare!). It was a pleasure to learn from you.

To all the ladies I'm connected to with healthy living, blogging, and food art! It is truly a pleasure to see all the beauty you put out into the world.

Jane, Alexa, and Lauren, who all helped bring the book together with their lovely photos.

To Leah, my editor, for taking a chance on me and helping me fulfill a dream.

To John Mack and Nate Hanson. You both inspire me . . . to laugh hard and to live fully. Thanks to both of you for your friendship and support.

ABOUT THE AUTHOR

Summer Sanders is the founder of Local Juicery, an all-organic superfood kitchen and pressed juicery located in Sedona, Arizona. She's a mama, health coach, blogger, and certified raw food chef. Summer is passionate about changing the way people relate to food by bringing awareness to organic, sustainable, and ethical practices. She loves creating food and tonics that taste as good as they are for you. She believes healthy food should taste amazing!

WEBSITE: strongandradiant.com
LOCAL JUICERY: localjuicery.com
FACEBOOK: facebook.com/strongandradiant
TWITTER: twitter.com/strong_radiant
INSTAGRAM: instagram.com/summer.sanders
PINTEREST www.pinterest.com/strongandradiant

INDEX

CONVERSION CHARTS

METRIC AND IMPERIAL CONVERSIONS
(These conversions are rounded for convenience)

Ingredient	Cups/Tablespoons/Teaspoons	Ounces	Grams/Milliliters
Butter	1 cup = 16 tablespoons = 2 sticks	8 ounces	230 grams
Cheese, shredded	1 cup	4 ounces	110 grams
Cream cheese	1 tablespoon	0.5 ounce	14.5 grams
Cornstarch	1 tablespoon	0.3 ounce	8 grams
Flour, all-purpose	1 cup/1 tablespoon	4.5 ounces/0.3 ounce	125 grams/8 grams
Flour, whole wheat	1 cup	4 ounces	120 grams
Fruit, dried	1 cup	4 ounces	120 grams
Fruits or veggies, chopped	1 cup	5 to 7 ounces	145 to 200 grams
Fruits or veggies, puréed	1 cup	8.5 ounces	245 grams
Honey, maple syrup, or corn syrup	1 tablespoon	0.75 ounce	20 grams
Liquids: cream, milk, water, or juice	1 cup	8 fluid ounces	240 milliliters
Oats	1 cup	5.5 ounces	150 grams
Salt	1 teaspoon	0.2 ounce	6 grams
Spices: cinnamon, cloves, ginger, or nutmeg (ground)	1 teaspoon	0.2 ounce	5 milliliters
Sugar, brown, firmly packed	1 cup	7 ounces	200 grams
Sugar, white	1 cup/1 tablespoon	7 ounces/0.5 ounce	200 grams/12.5 grams
Vanilla extract	1 teaspoon	0.2 ounce	4 grams

OVEN TEMPERATURES

Fahrenheit	Celsius	Gas Mark
225°	110°	¼
250°	120°	½
275°	140°	1
300°	150°	2
325°	160°	3
350°	180°	4
375°	190°	5
400°	200°	6
425°	220°	7
450°	230°	8